A
Perfectly Good
Fantasy

ALSO BY LYNN WALKER

Midnight Calling: A Memoir of a Drug Smuggler's Daughter
The award-winning prequel to *A Perfectly Good Fantasy*.

Breaking Midnight: A True Story

The story of her dad's life as an undercover narc-
turned-smuggler.

For updates on her fourth book, follow Lynn:

www.LynnWalkerMemoir.com

or on most social media: **@WalkerMemoir**

A Perfectly Good Fantasy

A MEMOIR

LYNN WALKER

MZW
PUBLISHING
Washington
USA

As with all memoirs, this book was recreated from memory. The author
has depicted incidents and conversations as accurately as possible. In
some cases she compressed events or reconstructed dialogue to reflect the
essence of what was said. Names and some identifying details have been
changed to protect individuals' privacy.

The author is grateful for permission to reprint lyrics from "Love Makes
the World Go Round" by Drew Keriakedes @ 2010 Circus Contraption

Cover design: Mile 102 Designs
Author photo on back cover: Swoboda Photography

Print ISBN: 978-1-7378955-8-9
Ebook ISBN: 978-1-7378955-9-6

MZW Publishing
Washington USA
www.MZWPublishing.com

For Ella, Thank you for helping me to soar—
the real kind of soaring.

&

For Floyd, the best dad I never had.

I once was in love with a beautiful boy
Maybe it was in a dream
It's hard to discern what is real or alive
When nothing is as it would seem

But love makes the world go 'round
Or so I've been told and I think I believe it
And when we decide to enlighten the wise
The world will be happy again

Lyrics from "Love Makes the World Go Round" by Drew
Keriakedes @ 2010 Circus Contraption

•

Acknowledgments

I am forever grateful to the thousands of people—
some great friends and some I saw only once—
who shared their experience, strength and hope
with me in twelve-step recovery meetings over the
past few decades. Over and over, they saved me
from the grip of addiction and helped me learn
how to live life on life's terms. A great deal of the
wisdom in this book, if readers find any, comes
from the addiction recovery community.

ONE

A Clean Slate

The hot wind is whipping our hair around, and the road noise is battering our eardrums, muffling everything but the howling from the backseat. We're just like Thelma and Louise, minus all the men. And the convertible Thunderbird. We're like Thelma and Louise in a Geo Metro with no AC and no Brad Pitt. As for the howling, that's what Siamese cats do in a carrier on a four-day road trip across the country.

Mom and I left Ohio three days ago headed for Washington State where I will, finally, be attending graduate school. It took me eight years to get a college degree due to a little cocaine and alcohol addiction; okay, more like several years in which I snorted, swallowed and smoked any drugs I could get my hands on. But that's all behind me now.

For miles, we've been seeing signs for some kind of Earth Festival and decide to stop there for a much-needed

2 · A PERFECTLY GOOD FANTASY

break from the constant, *Breoowww! Breoowww!* from the backseat.

As we wander through rows of tie-dyed dresses, hand-made jewelry and hemp baskets, I catch whiffs of skunky marijuana wafting off the people selling their crafts. This is no Earth Fest; this is a Weed Fest. Weed was the one drug I didn't like, but the smell makes me want to get stoned. The part of my brain that is still trying to kill me starts in on me. *I bet pot won't make you paranoid anymore. It'll just mellow you out like these hippies. The stuff is harmless.*

Righhht, I tell my brain. Dad went to prison for smuggling twelve thousand pounds of the shit. Harmless.

Moving on to the next booth, I hope it's less aromatic. An older guy with a thinning, gray ponytail is selling leather goods and eyeing my mom. *Great.* He is totally Mom's type too. She always goes for men who are broken. I mean, we're all broken in some way, but Mom goes for the notably broken.

I'm not doing much better in the relationship department. I don't think I got all the pages of the instruction manual because my life is only starting to look okay and just around the edges. Don't look too closely, especially if I'm involved with a man. Definitely didn't get those pages.

Gray Ponytail, grinning from ear to ear, waves us into his booth, saying, "You two gotta be sisters." I roll my eyes. I got *that* page of the instruction manual. Let me explain something about my mom, which brings me back to Thelma and Louise. She looks a lot like Louise—or Susan Sarandon—

wears her hair in similar loose curls and has those heavy-lidded bedroom eyes, only Mom's eyes are green. Mom is no pushover either, but today she is light and breezy at the Weed Festival and doesn't shut Gray Ponytail down.

"We're not sisters," she says. "I'm her mother."

"No way!" He looks at me then back to her. Pointing at Mom, he says, "You look like someone who'd wear leather." I don't even want to know what that means. "I'll give you a good deal. What do you want? How 'bout these moccasins?"

She scans his items then shakes her head. "No, thanks. I already have a leather bikini." Then she flashes him a smile. Have you seen Susan Sarandon smile?

Gray Ponytail is speechless for a few beats, as am I. Then he holds his hands out to her, very prayerful-like. "Will you marry me? *Pleeease.*"

With that, she tosses her head back in laughter.

Not wanting to hear any more about leather or marriage or to smell any more skunk weed, I scoot Mom out of this so-called Earth Festival, poor Ponytail calling after us about how well his moccasins will go with her bikini.

Having not been around stoners for years, I don't realize how tense I am until I'm back in the car and my shoulders droop in relaxation. With the Weed Fest in my rearview mirror, I'm safe again. I'm strong and free and headed for my new life. There's power and joy in being young, the road and the world stretched out before me, especially with my mom, who I now know owns a leather bikini, riding shotgun.

On the last day of our trip, with seven hours to go, we plan to stop only once for a lunch break. Mom drives first, and I hold down the pages of Linda Goodman's *Love Signs*, the corners flapping in the wind, and read out loud about our recent men, what the problems were and what horoscope signs make better matches. Maybe the missing instructions are in this book.

"Okay, Mom, it says the best signs for you are Pisces and Scorpio because—"

"That can't be right. Your father was a Scorpio, and you know how *that* turned out."

"But you were crazy about him when you guys met, right?"

She gives me a quick driving-glance, a look that means, Really? Do you really want to go there? "Oh, honey ... I was twenty when I met your dad. Most women are crazy about him when they first meet him."

I turn back to the flapping pages of Goodman's instruction manual for true love. "Sorry, Mom. A Scorpio was your best bet. Says you'll understand each other completely." Finger holding my place there on the words, I look over at her. "Did you, at least, understand him?"

"Nobody understood your dad. He wouldn't let anybody in."

"Did he understand you?"

She purses her lips, thinking or choosing her words. There must be some unspoken code between divorced parents not to criticize each other in front of the children. Or parents understand that criticizing someone who gave you half your genes is the same as criticizing you. How can Mom rip on the man who gave me my nose and my chin, my disarming nature? Oh, shit, I think. I don't let people in either. Wonder if that's hereditary.

"He was really good at, what would I call that ... reading people," she says. "But he never asked how I felt or about personal stuff. Maybe when we were first married, but then he changed so much when he started working undercover. And that was only a few years after we married."

We both grow quiet. I've kept my distance from Dad for five years, and he has been out of Mom's life for fifteen. One day, she had a strapping undercover narc as a husband, and the next morning, she had a note in the mailbox. But somehow, here he is in this car. I can almost smell his Old Spice cologne, hear his smooth-talking banter and his belly laugh. The mere thought of Dad is bigger than life. He is a force.

"I still can't believe that son-of-a-bitch gave you cocaine." Guess the divorced parent code only goes so far.

Late that afternoon, the rural university town that will be my home for the next two years comes into view. Stoic, old university buildings are perched on a hill, some looking very medieval European with clock towers and round turrets and conical roofs. The cloudless sky is dazzling blue behind all that burnt-orange brick.

Mom and I spend our last two days together setting up

my studio apartment, which is half of the main floor of an old, two-story house painted the color of pumpkin pie. The other half of the downstairs and all of the upstairs make up two other apartments. My slice of the pie consists of two rooms connected by a tiny kitchen. When I lean over to peek into the small oven, my butt hits the refrigerator, and the bathroom door only opens halfway before hitting the toilet.

Despite Mom's insistence that I not skimp—she paid plenty when I was a teenager, mostly in heartbreak and fear—I let her buy me a mattress, no bed frame; a table and two chairs; a flimsy, particle-board desk and a wicker loveseat that is actually patio furniture. Wicker is ideal for my tiny apartment: it's portable, so I can carry it onto the wide porch, almost doubling my apartment's square-footage.

As I unpack the kitchen supplies, I hold up my cookbook. "Look what I found. We can make Grandma's cornbread tonight."

"Yes! With pork chops and gravy." Gravy and cornbread will be like a christening of my new life because I come from a long line of strong-willed, hillbilly women from the South, women who were midwives and bluegrass singers and still came home and made gravy every day—the good stuff, using the grease from the meat. When Mom bought a George Foreman Rotisserie, she thought it was pretty clever how it had that tray underneath to catch all the meat drippings for gravy. George would be *so* disappointed.

"Let's go get all the stuff," she says, grabbing her purse. "I want to get your kitchen stocked up with food before I leave." The "leaving" talk makes my throat tighten. At twenty-six, having my mother leave shouldn't be foreboding but during the worst days of my using, she was all I had. Her and these two cats. Well, Dad was still there, if you consider supplying me with unlimited cocaine "being there."

I must've gone pale or something because Mom pauses and smiles reassuringly. "You're gonna do fine here. You're ready for this."

I'm not sure that I'm ready, but I *am* sure it's time. Way past time. It's time to move on to the next phase of life, to be an independent, self-supporting adult. I'm starting over here with a clean slate. No one will know that I'm still trying to figure out this simple-for-everyone-else thing called life. No one in this town will know what it took for me to get here, and I don't mean the four-day road trip.

TWO

Gin and Tonics

The way I stroll onto the university campus, get shown to an office and start getting paid to teach classes, you'd think I was on some kind of natural progression and had this planned all along. Trust me, I'm sliding into home plate on my ass, years late, toe stretched as far as I can reach it.

Safe! yells life's umpire, his arms slicing the air in front of him and out to his sides.

I will share my office with Isabelle, who is willowy and sexy and very sure of herself. I'm intimidated. Apparently, she is also very flexible because she does ballet. Having already settled into the office, she is welcoming and friendly. When she offers me a cup of hot tea, I'm completely disarmed. I'm such a pushover.

My graduate advisor, Dr. McKee, and I have our first meeting to strategize how I will master the field of environmental conflict resolution. He is pretty laid-back and insists that I call him Don. Since he is just starting his tenure, I guess he'd be in his early thirties, but his balding head makes him look older. His desk is a scattered mess: piles of books, stacks of papers, file folders sliding danger-ously near the edge, three coffee mugs, all dirty. Dr. McKee —Don—tells me that since my field of study is brand new, I'll have to piece together relevant courses from different departments. And I'll need to build an advisory committee with faculty from these departments. He rattles off a list of professors I should meet with from political science and sociology. I might want to get some training too, like in mediation; maybe the department can help pay for it. I'm scribbling furiously. His thinking is just like his desk: scattered.

I'm totally energized and excited and, at the same time, feel like a fraud, like I'm pretending to be a young, budding professional with goals and plans. If Don only knew about my past, he'd yank that teaching assistantship right out from under me and send me pack-ing. No, I remind myself. I'm a completely different person. I deserve to be here. I earned this position. And, if grad school doesn't work out, I can always go back to doing medical transcription, preferably at a psychiatric hospital, since I know all the terminology from the eight years that I worked at one. Wonder if I should be worried that I'm more comfortable in a psychiatric ward than in graduate school.

A couple of weeks into graduate school, a handful of students are hanging out in the breakroom talking about going out for drinks. I'm invited. Everyone is. My armpits prickle with sweat. What did I think was going to happen? Everyone drinks. Everyone drank when we weren't even of legal drinking age, wherever we could. Dorm rooms. Frat parties. Bars where we wouldn't get carded. But here I am with a bunch of students of legal drinking age. Of course, they're going out for drinks, it's Friday night. I am not going to a bar; I'll spend my weekend studying. My mind is racing for a good excuse not to go but comes up blank. *Now* my devious brain freezes up? I mumble something about having other plans.

Back at my apartment, my brain won't shut up. *You should go ... get to know the other students ... make some new friends.*

I ignore my thoughts and start dinner. While the pasta is cooking, I eat a scoop of ice cream. Mom stocked my freezer with a few pints of our favorite: Häagen-Dazs Swiss Chocolate Almond. Spoonful after spoonful distracts me from my mind and the other students and the bar that I'm *not* going to. Instead, I'm occupied with rich, sweet vanilla and roasted, crunchy almonds surrounded by dark, velvety chocolate. Who needs new friends?

After dinner, I'm still edgy about my peers who are out drinking, while I'm sitting in my apartment, alone. Except for the Siamese. *Oh, god. I'm becoming a cat lady.*

I flick on my little TV and click through the five or six

channels my antenna can pick up. Nothing good. I leave the TV on for the noise and begin pacing. I could study, but I already did hours of research today on potential thesis projects. I could go down to this Rico's Pub where the other students were headed. Stop in and say hi. Have a cup of hot tea.

Bad idea, I think.

The trying-to-kill-me part of my brain says, Actually, that's a lovely idea.

I get the Swiss Chocolate Almond back out and, leaning against the counter, polish it off straight from the pint. *Mmm*, bliss. The creamy, crunchy, sweet and toasty mingling in my mouth again—they should rename this Bliss Chocolate Almond. The ice cream is a great distraction from the bar that I am *not* going to. The cats are staring in silent judgment at me with their satin blue eyes. If it didn't prove that I was a pathetic cat lady, I'd say to them, Hey, sometimes humans eat for reasons other than hunger.

Trying to avoid their judgy looks, I start pacing the apartment again, but my place is so tiny, from their kitchen vantage point, the cats can see me wherever I go. In my next pivot at the desk, the local *Yellow Pages* that Mom picked up somewhere catches my eye. Flipping it open, I start scrolling for a phone number. When my finger lands on a hotline number for twelve-step recovery groups, I release a huge sigh of relief.

Someone answers the phone and tells me there's a

meeting at eight p.m. In thirty minutes. Hope surges. The location is at a church a short walk from my apartment. Good. Walking will occupy more of my time and settle my nerves.

As I near the church, my body relaxes some, and my mind grows quiet with the thought of sitting in the familiar, comfortable space of a recovery meeting. I recall the people who helped me get sober five years ago, feel the bittersweet tug of missing them and being grateful for them. Addiction recovery is like narrowly escaping a burning building. You're collapsed outside the building, clinging to others who also made it out. Sometimes, you grab hands and race back into the inferno to help someone else get out alive.

I smile, remembering Lori, who kept steering me away from the men, reminding me I was at meetings to get clean and sober, not to get laid. And sour-faced, old Jerry, a self-described motha fuckin' alcoholic. He told me to keep goin' to meetin's, no matter what. I don't care if your ass falls off out West, he said. Just pick it up and take it to a meetin' with you. Got that? I got it, I assured him.

Here I am, ass in hand. Up ahead is the building where the meeting is located, and out front is a gaggle of young college kids. They're all laughing and talking, some smoking cigarettes. In Ohio, I attended groups in the city where there was a mix of hard-edged women, grumpy old men, doctors, hard core guys right out of prison, middle-aged folks, young people who were broken and lost like me and everything in between. Everyone out front of this group looks nineteen or twenty and ... well put-together. How can these college kids help me?

Almost right in front of the building now, some of their words drift over to me: something about flunking a class and the worst teacher. *Ughh. They're all students. What if one of them is in the class I teach?* I don't want anyone in my department to know about my past. That would muddy my clean slate.

Their cigarette smoke reaches me now—the smell of burning paper and tobacco and ashes. I gave up smoking four years ago, but the memory is visceral: one draw will instantly settle my nerves. Sweet relief without any calories. Cigarettes were also great at shutting down my brain. And leaving my breath tasting like a wet ashtray and making me go through nicotine withdrawal, again. No, thanks. A cigarette might be the one thing these kids have that I want, but I'm not about to start smoking again. Quitting was too hard.

I could walk up and tell them how worried I am that I'll start drinking again, that I'm new here, so no one knows how dangerous it would be if I went to a bar. Out of the corner of my eye, I glance at the cluster of students. They look bubbly, as if none of them lost *their* virginity at fourteen in a broken-down car. But what do I know; they *are* attending a twelve-step meeting. People don't go to these meetings because their lives are fabulous.

Decide, I tell myself. Turn right or go straight. Right or straight. Pick. Another glance, then my gaze flits back down to the street. There go my feet, walking right past the church, right past the college kids who have nothing but nicotine to offer me, right past my flutter of hope.

As I continue walking, I feel floaty and not in a good way, in a drifty way. For years, I leaned hard into the recovery program. Those groups were where I was safe and connected—huddled with my comrades at the edge of the inferno. Walking away from this meeting is a little like pulling a plug, disconnecting myself from what has been a lifeline.

My feet seem to be on autopilot, on the way to where, I don't know. Somehow, they know to take me back to my apartment. I want to call Mom but don't want to worry her, and the mere thought of her voice, two thousand miles away, causes loneliness to swell inside me until I feel like I could choke. If I hear her voice, I will cry. That, I don't need.

Instead, I call Logan, my friend in Ohio who is always up late because, even when he takes his meds, he has low-grade mania. Early in our recovery—always the best time to get into a relationship—we started fooling around, until I realized I needed his friendship way too much to destroy it with sex.

"Hey, lady. How's it goin'?" Logan always sounds so happy to hear from me. I like that in a friend. In the background, I hear him lightly strumming his electric guitar. I smile at the image of how his hands are always moving.

"Not so good. I don't think I'm gonna make it out here—"

"What d'you mean? You just got there. You're not drinkin' already, are you?"

"No but ... everyone went to a bar tonight. That's gonna be a regular thing, I can tell. Everyone drinks. I tried to go to a meeting, but it was a bunch of preppy college kids."

"Maybe you should try a different meeting. There's gotta be some sober, crusty ol' geezers somewhere."

"I don't know. This is a pretty small town with a big university. Lots of bars and students."

"You ain't got no business in a bar. You know that's not gonna end well." I listen to the faint guitar sounds streaming through the line. "Probably end great for some lucky guy, though," he says, chuckling.

He plays me his new song, which is really good: rambling and melancholy then burning and intense. Pretty much epitomizes Logan. After chatting for another fifteen minutes, I say goodnight before my long-distance phone bill gets outrageous. It's not even ten p.m., too early to go to bed, but that seems like the safest bet.

The rest of the weekend, I work from home, good cat lady that I am. Also, a good way to avoid the department and another invite.

Sunday afternoon, I'm sitting on the porch with a cup of hot tea. It's one of those chilly, crisp days that only occur in the fall. The yard is dappled with sunlight filtering through a giant maple tree, leaves fringed with scarlet, a beautiful, violent contrast: green leaves bleeding. This tree is ready for Halloween. My upstairs neighbor thumps down the stairs with her lunch and sits in one of two chair that appeared on the porch Friday evening when I was out *not* getting help from preppy college kids.

We introduce ourselves. Heather and her husband, Eric, are both working on their PhDs in counseling and psychology. Great, I think, a couple of shrinks. They'll see right through me. She plans to become a school counselor. As I talk with her, that seems like an ideal job for here, as she is disarming and completely non-judgmental. She has these big, chocolate drop eyes that are so dark they seem to absorb everything I say. Heather listens even with her eyes. I believe she'd sit here and let me talk for hours, and nothing I say would faze her. That is, if I told her even half the truth about me, which I don't.

After our lunch, we go upstairs where she introduces me to her cats and her husband, in that order. I like this lady. She has two all-black kitties. They match her two dark eyes, I think. Her husband, Eric, is the exact opposite of her (and their cats): strawberry blonde hair, freckles and pale, blue eyes. He is shy and polite and clearly smitten with Heather, not a flirty bone in his body. I like that in a girlfriend's husband.

Turns out Eric is in experimental psychology, no interest whatsoever in working with people. *Phew!* I won't worry about him analyzing me or picking up on any of my, hopefully, well-concealed dysfunction. Wonderful.

"What kind of experiments are you doing?" I ask.

"I'm researching drug addiction."

Oh. So wonderful.

He tells me all about his research and how he studies drug addiction with rodents. Using cocaine. How does he manage to stay away from the coke? He continues talking, but I have stopped listening because my brain has latched onto the fact that my upstairs neighbor has access to pharmaceutical grade cocaine. It's probably even better than Dad's uncut Colombian stuff. I snap out of my reverie when Eric starts talking about how the rats self-administer the drug by hitting a bar, choosing hits of cocaine even over food. You don't say!

I don't tell Eric anything about *my* previous research self-administering cocaine.

The next weekend, Heather and Eric invite me to bring my dinner upstairs and eat with them. She, no doubt, senses that I'm homesick and lonely; good school counselors have a knack for detecting loneliness. When I arrive, Eric is making gin and tonics and offers me one, which I promptly decline.

"Here you go, sweetie," he says in a sing-song voice, setting a gin and tonic with ice and a wedge of lime in front of Heather. The glass looks frosty cold, sweating and dripping.

She gives three quick little air kisses in his direction and takes a sip. "*Mmm.* This is a yummy one."

We have a lighthearted evening, laughing and getting to know each other. They each drink exactly one of those classy gin and tonics. Heather giggles about how sometimes she'd like a second one, but they like to make a bottle of gin last a month. Or some crazy shit like that.

As I'm bopping down the stairs back to my place, I'm full of gratitude for my newfound friends—so healthy and fun—and for the fact that I drank not one of those classy gin and tonics.

My brain, on the other hand, is appalled. *That there was a waste of perfectly good alcohol.*

THREE

Normal People

E ventually, I also befriend the downstairs neighbors: three graduate students from Germany, the UK and India. Gretchen sunbathes topless on the sunny side of the front lawn, tsking in disgust about the horny American men who keep gawking at her. George complains about how US beer tastes like water and gawks at Gretchen when she sunbathes. Sunita is talkative and funny and exotically beautiful, with thick, shiny black hair to her waist. At twenty-two, she has never seriously dated a man because that isn't really acceptable where she comes from, the boys and girls segregated all the way through high school. Having been preoccupied with men since I hit puberty, or since Dad walked out on us, I can't even conceive of such a life. What did she do in high school and college? Apparently, she studied, spent time with female friends and family, cooked, traveled, went to movies. Well, there are those activities.

My new neighbors and I frequently cross paths on our shared porch coming and going from classes. Five of us— George is usually out hiking, rock climbing or looking for Guinness beer—often have dinner together, toting our food to the apartment of whoever is hosting that evening, since none of us have enough money to make food for everybody. We still eat, sort of, potluck style with everybody trying bites of each other's dishes. One evening, Sunita makes mango lassis, and I wonder how I lived this long without tasting such a heavenly treat: creamy and sweet with a tangy, tropical, slightly flowery flavor.

This must be what normal people do in grad school.

After a month or so, I can't invent any more respectable reasons not to go out with the students from my department. Rico's Pub is a funky little bar full of other students and a few crusty, ol' geezers—Logan was right, there are a few in this town. They're at the bars. As I take in the smoky room, it dawns on me that this is the first time I've been in a bar while of legal drinking age. When I sobered up two months before my twenty-first birthday, my brain gave me no end of shit. *Are you kidding? You're stopping now, when you can walk right into any bar you want and get a drink. Don't quit now; the fun is just beginning.* In the end, I told my addicted brain to shut the hell up because being underage never stopped me from getting a drink and because drinking hadn't been fun for a long, long time.

Here I am at Rico's, five years later, having a scarily similar internal conversation. *Wow, I can walk right up to*

the bar and order anything I want, which is tequila—I mean,
would be tequila. If I still drank. Which I don't.

"What can I getcha?" the bartender asks.

I stare at him for a few seconds. Bottle of Coors, I
think. Or one of those draft beers, please. No tequila. Luckily, the next thought from the small part of my brain that
isn't trying to kill me is, Do you remember what happened
the last time you drank booze? You don't? Exactly.

Other people are jostling around me, antsy to get their
orders in, so I order a soda water with lime, hoping no one
around me heard that. The bartender doesn't even raise an
eyebrow. Nothing fazes a bartender; they've seen it all.
Even soda water with lime.

At our table, everyone drinks their beers, and I sip my
bubbly water, which may look like a gin and tonic but sure
doesn't taste like one. Mostly, I ignore being the only one
not drinking booze. Over and over, I ignore my thoughts of
how easily I could walk up to the bar and order any drink I
want.

Instead, I focus on my peers, getting to know them.
This is a skill I learned from Miriam, the therapist I saw
when I was between the ages of twenty and twenty-six.
I've found this "getting to know people" thing comes in
very handy for, say, making friends. If I ask lots of questions about *them*, I can avoid or postpone questions about
me—people love to talk about themselves. Talking about
my life is complicated. Do I tell the truth? Share the light
version? Leave out the worst parts? Turns out, if I leave out
drug abuse, getting arrested, being a ward of the juvenile

court, having a psycho boyfriend and an unplanned pregnancy, I had a pretty good life.

Tonight, I spend the evening getting to know the other students, emphasis on them. Patrick is a skinny, pale, almost sickly looking man who is new here from outside of Boston. He is very quiet and seems a bit uncomfortable or awkward. At least he has a beer, which he has been nursing for an hour. A social drinker.

Samuel is from Malawi, Africa. He is boisterous and drinks very heavily. I like him right away. He pulls out his wallet to show me pictures of his wife and two boys, the family that he couldn't afford to bring with him to the States. After he points to his boys' faces and tells me their names, he leaves his fingertips resting on the photo, staring at their smiling faces for a long moment. I doubt my father carries photos of my brother and me in his wallet. I watch as Samuel tenderly tucks his boys back into his wallet.

"You have kids?" he asks me, his voice sounding raspy with sadness.

That's an easy question. "No. No kids yet."

"*Hmm.*" He looks at me, contemplating, his lips pursed. "How old are you now?"

"Twenty-six." Never had a problem with this question either.

"You better get started on that before you're too old." He starts, literally, wagging his finger at me, disapproving. "My wife and I had our first baby at twenty-two."

"*Hah!* I'm not too old. Lots of women don't start families until they're in their thirties. Least, here in the States."

He starts tsking and tongue clicking, shaking his head. "No, no. Listen to me. You have to find a husband—you are not married yet, right?"

I shake my head and take a sip of my soda water. So refreshing and relaxing.

"First the husband." He holds up his index finger, not wagging this time, just counting. "This can take a while, yes? Then, having babies"—a second finger goes up—"this can take some time too. Know what I mean?"

I know exactly what he means. The whole impossible matter has been on my mind for years because I always wanted kids, but not without an acceptable husband, which I can't seem to find. "I'm not in any hurry, but thanks for your advice." I smile at Samuel.

"No problem. I can give you free advice. Anytime." He extends his arms, looks around the bar. "And if you want, I can fix you up with some nice man."

Glancing around the room, I look back at him and start to respond. "Uh, I don't—"

Watching my reaction, he bursts out laughing. "I'm only joking. A man you meet in a bar, this is not a good husband for you."

Don't I know.

Anne, an opinionated, second-year graduate student, sits across the table from me. She is drinking near-beer because, she blurts out to everyone, she's a recovering alcoholic. This is great news, I think, a comrade. It gives me a flash of hope. But I'm floored that she can, so nonchalantly, spout off that she's an alcoholic. And drinking near-beer? I was cautioned to avoid that stuff, alcohol is alcohol, and it could trigger a craving for the real stuff. Why anyone would drink near-beer is beyond me: watered-down beer with no effect unless you drown in the stuff. What, does it taste good or something?

Anne never stops talking and is a self-described "alpine urban" woman, which she says means that she grew up in the city, Seattle, but spent every chance she could backpacking in the mountains. She then proceeds to tag all of us. Patrick is straight "urban," she says, from a big city on the East Coast. She labels Clint as a "mountain man," which seems spot-on: full beard, a man of few words, hiking boots, flannel shirt, hunter. I'm a "nouveau alpine," a mid-West transplant who came west for the mountains. She skips Samuel, possibly because she knows nothing about Malawi and doesn't want to be offensive. I give Anne my own private label: "alpine narcissist."

Maybe *this* is what normal people do in grad school.

Ninety minutes and two soda waters later, I excuse myself to get home. Mountain-man Clint offers to walk me home.

First alcohol and now a man. Must I avoid all vices tonight?

Technically, I'm still involved with Scott, a wickedly smart psychologist-in-training at the hospital where I worked before grad school. We're seeing how our relationship goes living halfway across the country and agreed to be honest if either of us wants to date someone else. Clint is not a qualifying "someone else." Scott can melt me with his smile, and those lips—he is a great kisser. And his understanding of human anatomy makes him an amazing lover. Unfortunately, his understanding of the human psyche makes him cautious and a bit uneasy about by my past, the little he knows of it. Since I moved two thousand miles away, Scott is only a voice over the phone line—a sexy voice—and still supporting in me and cracking me up. He has a great sense of humor, for a psychologist. I'm trying to stay attached through our weekly calls, but my heart has taken cover, preparing for the end by being partway gone already.

Yes, avoid all vices tonight, I decide and wisely pass on Clint's offer to walk me home. I don't plan on relapsing tonight, on booze or men. As I weave my way through the crowded bar to the front door, I glance back at our table. Clint gives me a smile and a good-bye nod. Anne tosses her head back at something and her cackle cuts through even the din of a bar on Friday night in a college town.

I push the door open. The fresh air washes over me, clearing my head.

Safe! life's umpire shouts.

FOUR

Full Sail into the Wind

W e're at Rico's. This *is* what normal people do in grad school on Friday night. This is any Friday in any college town. Except tonight, I notice every single beer my friends order: dark, amber colored beer with heads of thick, dense foam. This is no Coors. Full Sail Amber, they say, a microbrew. Blank look from me. Made in small batches, they say. I conjure the Budweiser brewery in my home town—huge building, multiple silver stacks, clouds of yeasty steam billowing from them. The smell always made my mouth water. Tonight, I'm zoomed in on every foamy microbrew my friends consume. These Full Sails are beacons: bright, unavoidable, swirling perpetually in my view. Beacons on a rocky cliff. I notice each beer the way someone with an eating disorder notices every morsel of food. I can tell who is tipsy (Clint), who is drunk (Samuel, always) and who is trying hopelessly to get tipsy (Anne).

Soda water won't cut it tonight. I order a diet soda. Really pushing the limits here. This isn't fair, I think, sipping my diet. I wanna try one of those microbrews. No tequila; definitely no tequila. No, no, no. No microbrew either. Another diet, please. At least I can get a caffeine buzz, so I'm not the only one who is straight.

After his third beer in two hours—but who's counting?—Clint leans across the table. "I'm gettin' another beer. You want one?" He smiles, glowing sweet with a buzz but still not drunk. He doesn't seem like the type to overindulge in anything; he's more like an easy flowing stream than a torrent. I know this because I can immediately assess a man's character, mood and intoxication level using some serious hypervigilance that, seemingly, resides inside me. This vigilance was acquired during the four years in high school I spent with Mark, my psychotic, drug-dealing boyfriend. Post-Traumatic Stress Disorder, I suppose, but to me it just feels like an uptight, over-worked, deranged CIA agent living in my head. Tonight, my internal agent informs me that Clint is a gentle man in every way.

What Clint is asking me is the most dangerous question in the world.

Do I want a beer? Hell, yes, I want one. But only one. This is the first time that thought—just one beer—isn't followed by a recollection of other times I decided to have "just one" then plowed through a six-pack. Or more. This is the first time I don't think about losing my five plus years of sobriety. The first time I don't put a few beats between the thought of a beer and my actions.

A little flutter comes alive in my stomach, an innocent little butterfly of excitement, which should be a warning bell clanging. Or a siren wailing. I doubt normal drinkers get butterflies when they ponder whether or not to have a beer. They either want one or they don't. But asking an alcoholic if they want a drink is like asking a gambler if they want a free trip to Vegas.

Ten weeks after I started my new life in graduate school, ten weeks after I walked past the college kids in front of that recovery meeting, five years after I last snorted cocaine with my father, I smile at Clint and say, "Sure. I'll have one."

My eyes follow him all the way to the bar and all the way back to our table, willing him not to slop any beer out of the pints in each hand. I'm laser locked onto that pint and am salivating. Already, I can feel the dense foam that the beer is going to leave on my upper lip, can almost taste the yeasty flavor as I lick the foam off my lip. Clint hasn't even sat the pint glass in front of me yet, and I am lit up. I'm pretty sure normal drinkers don't fantasize about practically having oral sex with a beer.

In the past, I was no fan of beer. I drank hard liquor and without any mixers—let the stuff get right to work in my body with the least amount of time, volume and calories. But this beer is no Coors. Or even a Heinekens. This is rich and strong, nutty and almost bitter. I want to chug it straight down. Another alarm should be blaring. I am consuming it as quickly as I can without drawing any attention, which isn't easy because tonight Clint is very attentive.

Sitting between Anne and I, Clint rarely looks in her direction. He chats me up about how I liked Ohio State University and the inevitable question about the Buckeyes. I explain that I never went to a Buckeyes football game. No, not one. From his incredulous head shake, I gather he loves football. That's too bad.

Shifting in his chair, Clint turns completely in my direction, his back to Anne. Looks like my lack of appreciation for football, even the Buckeyes, is no deterrent. Poor Anne, I know how she prefers everyone's attention on her. While I'm trying to match my drinking pace to Clint's, which is frustratingly slow, he starts talking hunting. I wonder if he is always this romantic.

"Uh ... I grew up in the city. No hunting. That I knew of. Did a lot of fishing. And target shooting."

He lights up at that. "What kind of guns?"

"Handguns. Dad was a cop, so he taught us when we were little, like four and six."

"Really? Where'd you grow up?"

Here we go. This is where I start filtering my life. "Miami. Dad was a narc."

Blank stare.

Surely, they have narcs in Idaho. Or did he say he was from Montana? "An undercover narcotics agent," I clarify.

"Cool. Like Miami Vice?"

I always get that one. "Only not that glamorous. Least

that's what Dad always said." Comparing the level of beer in his glass to the level in mine, I take a gulp. "So, what do you hunt with?"

He goes on and on about what powered rifles he uses for which kind of prey. Killing animals ... this isn't something men should talk about with a woman they're getting to know. As far as bar chats go, this is one of the most violent, and dullest. At least, that I can remember. Maybe that's why I used to black out—boring conversations.

When I come back to the table with another Full Sail, I chat with some of the other students to put a pause on the cozy, manly-man talk with Clint.

My body isn't used to the effects of alcohol anymore, and that second Full Sail puts a little wind in my sails. A warm, balmy wind like those that blew our sailboat in the Florida Keys, while my father trimmed the sails. I'm sailing tonight, right back to the bar where I order a third beer.

By the time I sip-chug that beer, I forget all about drinking's rocky cliff of oblivion. My fellow students are my best friends. Even Anne is my buddy tonight. My future is so full of promise and fun and adventure, I could explode with joy. I can see it all stretched out ahead of me, wide open like the horizon in the Keys. A career dealing with environmental conflicts, maybe I'll end up in law school and become an environmental attorney. I'll be sought out by the likes of The Nature Conservancy and The Wilderness Society. I'll have a handsome, funny, trustworthy husband and a couple of happy kids—a life-long dream. At last, I will have the good parts of life.

The next morning, my head is a little fuzzy but not splitting in pain like the old days. I'm elated to be able to recount the entire evening. I only drank three beers—I actually kept track—before everyone started to leave. Clint walked me home, but I didn't invite him in or kiss him goodnight. Scott is still my boyfriend, and I was on my best behavior.

Things are going to be different this time. I'm a grown-up. I'm drinking legally. I had a little trauma when I was a kid and later when Dad shared his cocaine with me. But that's all behind me now. There's nothing wrong with having a beer once in a while. With friends. To unwind.

My mind lands on that over and over throughout the following weeks: I can drink normally. Once or twice a week, I take my drinking-normally confidence right to the bar, where I unwind. With a few beers and a few friends. I never drink alone, and I never drink tequila. Right after cocaine, tequila was my drug of choice. Both hit my blood-stream fast and kicked-in hard—*Bam!*—exactly the way I liked it. I'm avoiding both.

I don't tell anyone who knows about my past drug and alcohol abuse—Mom, Logan, Miriam, Floyd (Mom's brother)—that I'm drinking again. Irrelevant information because alcohol isn't a problem anymore. Having a few beers is not a big deal, not a big part of my life, and I don't want anyone worrying. I definitely don't tell Scott; he never witnessed my past and is still afraid of it. Not Logan because it might destroy our bond.

Logan is the only person from my old recovery group with whom I maintain contact. In early recovery, we were like littermates—after we stopped having sex—both blinded by addiction and rooting around for a lifeline. Logan and I, with a few other young people also devastated by addiction, spent hours at Denny's drinking coffee loaded with sugar, eating onion rings, talking, laughing, bullshitting and sometimes getting honest. Partly, we were doing what all the other twenty-somethings were doing: staying out half the night. Mostly, we were keeping each other safe until the bars closed.

I finally get honest with Logan during one of our late-night, guitar-rambling calls, confessing that I'm drinking again. He doesn't judge me. He simply receives my confession with compassion and absolves me of all sin. I like that in a recovering addict.

"I think I got it under control," I assure him.

"That's good. Wish I could do that. If I started again, next thing you know, I'd be out there slammin' cough syrup and washin' it down with Old English forty-ouncers."

"And getting depressed again." I don't say what we're probably both thinking: and getting suicidal. "Yeah, please don't do that."

"Oh, I have no intention of doing that again. No fuckin' way. I won't make it back." Soft guitar melody in the background. "So, what d'you think, you weren't really an addict or what?"

"I don't know. To be honest, I don't think much about it," I lie. "Every once in a while, I have a beer. Guess I just needed to get my shit together."

He hoots. "You think? Well, if you lose your shit again, you can always go back to meetings."

Only I am not going to lose my shit. And I am not going back to meetings. I got this under control.

FIVE

A Few Important Reminders

On a long weekend, my uncle, Floyd, and I head into the Pasayten Wilderness for three days of backpacking. Two of the main reasons I applied for graduate school in Washington were to be near Floyd, who has been like a father to me—the best father I never had—and to be near the mountains.

After working one summer as a wilderness ranger, I began to crave mountains like I used to crave a drink. The mountains ground me and make me right-sized in the world. They make me want to live deliberately and not stumble through life in a drunken stupor. Lately, I'm in need of such reminders.

At the trailhead, a gray, jagged mountain peak, covered still with pockets and crevasses of snow, looms in the distance. The peak is harsh—fissured and crumbling from glaciers that retreated and advanced, scouring it for eons. Tonight, that mountain is our destination.

Floyd ties a bandana over his head to keep his bald head from burning, while I unload our backpacks from the trunk. His pack is so heavy, I have to use both my arms to even lift it. A stocky, muscular man—probably has sixty pounds on me—he can handle a heavier pack, but I have no idea why his pack is so heavy for such a short trip.

"*Geez*," I say, "I can barely lift this beast. My pack's at least thirty-five pounds. Yours must be what, fifty? What'd you bring, a cast iron skillet?"

"No, but I do have a Subway sandwich in there."

I shake my head in mock disappointment, and he laughs. He probably does have a Subway in there. Since he got divorced several years ago and my cousin went to college, he's become such a workaholic bachelor, even eating carry-out for breakfast.

He gives our packs a comparative lift, one in each hand, tipping like a scale, first to one side, then the other. "Hey, mine *is* a lot heavier than yours, you need to carry the skillet." He plops my pack at my feet and grins. "Or we have to switch packs."

I let out a snort. "God, I'd die carrying your pack." I continue razzing him about what he has in there while we hoist on our packs and cinch down the straps until our packs are comfortable. What am I saying, comfortable? We adjust the packs so none of the straps are biting into our muscles yet.

"I do have my Glock and some ammo in here," he finally says. "That adds a few pounds."

Of course, his gun. My uncle is the most gentle,

tender-hearted man I know. He stopped hunting when he was a teenager after he shot a rabbit that didn't die from the first shot. One look at that suffering, and he was done. But Floyd works with the Seattle police helping them deal, often at night, with mentally ill people. After being held-up one evening at gunpoint, he got his concealed carry permit. He carries a gun in the wilderness in case of a bear encounter. Even I carry my .38 Special—a gift from my godfather, Bob—when I backpack alone, though I do so in case of encounters with wild men.

The trail starts off following a creek, the water raging too loudly for us to talk. Surveying the forest, I'm proud to identify every tree around us, thanks to my newly acquired undergrad degree. The lowest branches of the massive red cedar trees droop at forty-five-degree angles almost to the forest floor, the feathery branchlets forming a lacy dress around the trunk. This forest is like a fancy ball, a prom, the only one I've ever been to.

As we climb up and away from the creek, I hear bird songs from every direction. My calves burn with the stretch and strain of the steep trail and my breathing is labored. The rugged terrain is taunting me, challenging me to go on, which energizes me. Just try and tell me I can't do something. The wilderness is one place where my stubbornness and strong will is an asset. My first reminder: don't let anything stand in the way of reaching a goal, even if—especially if—it seems unattainable. Never give up. Tonight, I *am* sleeping next to a cloud-hidden alpine lake.

The trail switches back on itself with a sharp left turn, then right, then left again, each stretch only ten feet higher than the last one. Our progress is imperceptible, a crawl. It's still better than hiking straight uphill, which *would* require crawling. After an hour of switchbacks and carefully picking our way over and around roots and rocks, I pant out, "Remind me—why do we—do this?"

Floyd lets out a short-of-breath chuckle. "We like—self-inflicted—pain?"

"Exactly," I groan.

"What—you're not—having fun?"

My legs are cramping with exhaustion and my shoulders scream where the straps dig in, but I *am* having fun. Damn it. I am in my element. I'm where I most want to be. Looking down into the yawning valley below us, I can see how far we have actually climbed in only a few hours. Reminder number two: it helps to, occasionally, look back at how far you've come but don't linger too long; it makes the journey ahead seem impossible or, worse, makes your current location suddenly "good enough." Just keep trudging.

An hour later, we reach a ridge with a sweeping view of the mountain whose peak has been spying on us all day. The mountainside is covered with boulders, crushed rocks and scree punctuated with clumps of dark green conifers that somehow survive—stubborn trees—on the barren, steep slope. The mountain forms a craggy bowl around a lake—a flash of sapphire in the sun.

Floyd and I pause to take it all in, also known as

resting and catching your breath. The late afternoon sun is beating down on us, my shirt is soaked with sweat and clinging to my skin, my legs are trembly. But the view is worth every grueling step.

It takes us thirty minutes to carefully pick our way down to the lake. When we reach it, I want to tear off my damp, chaffing pack and drop the thirty-five-pound hunk to the ground. But we still have to find a good campsite—level, without rocks or roots that will jab us while we sleep, and close enough to the lake to collect water but far enough that we won't contaminate it. No toilets out here. Lugging this pack for another several minutes while we search for a campsite seems unbearable. I want this weight off of my body, right now, right here. However, if I ditch my pack here and go find the perfect campsite, I will have to, then, leave this perfect campsite, walk all the way back here, hoist the pack onto my shoulders again and carry it all the way back to the campsite. A third reminder: a steady trudge, one foot in front of the other, is far more productive than stopping and starting, fits and starts.

And when you finally reach your destination, your perfect spot, make sure it's where you *truly* want to be—not where someone else wants you to be, not almost there, not close enough, but actually "there."

We find a perfect spot near the lake's outlet, where water gushes from the lake into a narrow streambed. Dropping my pack, at last, I walk around with a forward lean, the sensation that I could flip right over with all that weight off my back.

As frigid evening air settles around us, we change into polar fleece, pitch our tent and pull out our food bags. I glance over as Floyd slides out a flattened Subway sandwich.

And I thought there were McDonald's everywhere. I start laughing. "You *actually* brought a whole sub up here?"

"Nooo." He grins. "Only half of one. I like something fresh my first day in. Try it." He's unwrapped one end of the thing, which has been compacted down to about one inch thick, limp shreds of pale lettuce dangling.

I scrunch my nose. "It's all smashed."

He shrugs and extends it to me, eyebrows up in question.

"Fine." You don't have to push me too hard to eat anything after an eight-mile hike gaining 2,500 feet in elevation. Turns out a compressed sub tastes the same as a regular one. He brought chocolate chip cookies from Subway too, which are basically a bag of crumbs. Best crumbs I've had in years.

Stretched out near a small campfire, we sip hot cocoa and watch stars begin to speckle the darkening sky. "Got any ideas for your thesis yet?" Floyd asks.

"I'm really interested in water conflicts. They're happening everywhere now, all over the West."

"They're gonna get worse."

"That or maybe Russian nuclear power plants."

"What?" He sounds astonished. "Are you serious?"

"Yep. Doctor McKee hooked me up with a poli-sci

professor who's sending a couple of grad students to Russia. Next summer." I blow on my cocoa, take a sip. "Said I could go too. They've been working with a nuclear power plant there—"

"Whoa, that's pretty serious."

I take another sip, my cocoa cooling fast in the cold night air. "The plant had some leaks. Not as bad as Chernobyl, but ... it has the same kind of reactor. Some environmental groups have formed, protesting against the plant. Lots of conflict."

"So ... you'd go over and what ... interview all the groups?"

"Not sure. I've gotta talk more with my advisors. The whole thing feels pretty overwhelming. Maybe better for a PhD than a master's."

"Do you want a PhD?"

"Are you kidding? I still can't believe I graduated from college."

"You know, the only thing that can keep you from getting a—"

"I know, I know. The only thing that can stop me is myself. You said that about me going to college back when I was in high school."

"See? And now you're *teaching* college classes."

I do see. I see how my life turned on a dime, took a hundred-eighty-degree turn. I see that I can do just about anything I want. And I see thousands of stars salted across the night sky.

The Milky Way galaxy is visible—an inky ribbon of

stars and deep purple gases and stardust tangled in the dark above us. This is something I've mostly viewed in solitude while working as a wilderness ranger, private viewings of the vastness of the universe from tiny, infinitesimal spots on the Earth where I sat. A fourth reminder: I'm a mere speck of dust, here and gone in a blink.

It's nice, for a change, to share the universe with another dust speck by my side.

SIX

One and Only Chances

In the morning, I slip out of the tent to go pee. As I'm squatting near a tree, I spy several female deer browsing on a knoll above me, their ears twitching, their noses periodically lifting in the air. After I zip up my pants, I watch the deer. It's a healthy-looking herd, no scarred or lame deer, their winter coats growing thick. There are three older females and four yearlings.

Suddenly, the deer look down, not at me but to my left, then, in unison, their white tails shoot straight up and all seven bound up the hill and out of sight.

That was weird, I think, must be a buck nearby. That's what I should do next time I see a guy coming my way—bolt, that is, not stick my tail in the air. Scanning the area to my left, looking for the buck, I notice a rump sticking out from behind a tree about a hundred feet from me. Uhh, the fur on that rump is much longer and dark than deer fur. I lean forward. That rump is much larger than a deer's.

That is no deer rump. I take a tentative step to get a better view. My eyes slowly follow those brown hindquarters up, up, up, right to a hump over the shoulders ... of a bear. *A shoulder hump. Shit, shit, shit! It's a grizzly.*

The bear shifts its hulking body, and I hold my breath and move not one single muscle. My heart thumps so crazily in my chest, I feel like I'm going into cardiac arrest. The bear is slurping berries off the bushes, one after another, sloppy jowls jiggling and flopping as he twists his snout and chews the berries. *A grizzly having breakfast.* They are notoriously grumpy when their meals are disturbed, and I'm only a few lumbering bear-gallops from his dining area. The bear is oblivious to me. For now.

Moving as quietly as I can, I side-step back toward the tent, my eyes locked onto that rump jutting out from the base of the tree, willing it not to move in my direction, willing it to think only of berries and more berries. When the rump is out of sight, I still walk backwards and side-ways, as fast as I can without tripping, constantly watching for any sign of movement from the bear's direction. Still, no bear in sight and no rustling from any nearby bushes.

Scrambling into the tent—always a safe spot to hide from a grizzly—I whisper, "Floyd! Get up, get up. There's a bear out there."

He bolts upright, still inside his sleeping bag, and says out loud, "Don't whisper. Start talking. Loud."

"Right, right," I say loudly. "It's a grizzly. Eating berries."

"Sure it's a grizzly?" He reaches down to the foot of the tent and slides his hand under his hiking pants there.

I nod, then remember to be loud. Practically yelling. "Definitely. It's got a shoulder hump. He's eating berries." I point in the direction but Floyd isn't looking at me. He's sliding his Glock 10-millimeter out from under his pants, chambering a round.

He steps out of the tent. "Where was it?" he asks.

Still hunkered in the safety of our flimsy nylon tent, I stick my head out. "It's over there," I point. "About a hundred yards." The sight of Floyd scanning the area, Glock in hand, while barefoot and wearing white undies is hysterical. If I wasn't scared shitless, I would be snickering. I would snicker very loudly.

"It if shows up, you come and stand right next to me—"

"Right," I say, clamoring out of the tent. "Look big. Wave our arms. Shout." I know all of this from my ranger training. It's all coming back to me, flooding back into my mind. *Fuck!* Reminder number five: try not to backpack when menstruating. The bears can smell the blood.

"Can you even stop a grizzly with that?" I tip my chin at his gun.

"I'd hate to try. I'd shoot in the air first. Hope the noise scares it away." He looks at me with a not-too-sure grimace. "I don't see or hear anything. Let's pack our stuff, get our food bag and get out of here."

"Yeah! Let's get outta here."

We pack up as loudly and as bigly as we can, watching

for the grizzly. Not a grunt, huff or twig breaking from that direction. We sling on our packs and stomp our way up to the main trail, all the while chattering noisily and glancing in the bear's direction. Once we're back up on the trail and moving, we check behind us every few minutes. Eventually, Floyd holsters his gun.

Floyd has been backpacking for years, maybe ten or fifteen years longer than I have, and he's never seen a grizzly. I realize what a rare occurrence it is to see a wild grizzly up so close, perhaps a once in a lifetime event. Especially if the bear goes after you because that will likely be the last time you see a grizzly, or anything else. That gives me a knot in my stomach.

"Man, am I glad those deer alerted me," I say, letting out a huge, relieved gush of air.

"I'm glad you were paying attention!"

Exactly, I think. The grizzly could've mauled me. Or I could've missed the privilege of seeing him. One final reminder: pay attention, even in the wilderness or other places where you think there's little danger. Also, if you don't pay attention, you might miss a one and only chance.

SEVEN

Soaring

T o prove (to whom I don't know) that I don't have a problem anymore and don't need those recovery groups, I'm hyperfocused on controlling my drinking. I'm preoccupied with what I drink (beer is okay, no hard stuff), how many (four draft microbrews or five Coors) and how fast (if slowly, I can have five microbrews or six Coors). I never drive if I'm drinking. In all my classes, I maintain straight As—hard, cold evidence that I've got my shit together.

When I'm home for winter break, Scott and I see each other, and, as usual, he has a sweaty schedule lined up for us: indoor rock climbing, gym workouts, trail running if the snow is light, and some cool-down exercises in the bedroom. While I still love his company and our physical relationship, and we have a lot of fun together, I can feel us drifting apart. An athletic, endorphin-fueled love can't withstand a two-thousand-mile distance.

During our first phone call after I return, we discuss our situation and how we're feeling. I still adore and respect Scott, and his feelings for me are mutual, but we've grown apart. It makes sense that we start seeing other people, explore our options but stay friends. This was a well-thought-out breakup; nothing rash or impulsive was ever going to happen with this man. I have some sadness about our breakup, but I'm not shattered, which is telling. The difficult good-bye with him happened when I moved away several months ago.

In the following weeks, I find myself waffling about letting go of my relationship with Scott because he's a great catch: funny and smart and educated and cute. But, I keep my waffling to myself when we occasionally talk on the phone, which is less and less. I don't want to stir things back up with him because I know Scott isn't the man for me. I can never let it all hang out with him, "it" being my past, not my belly (which has never been firmer since falling in athletic love with him). Scott is also not too interested in marriage, and I'm not getting any younger.

Graduate school is as good a place as any to find a husband—hey, a girl can dream. So, now that I'm single again, as I work on my master's research, I start researching husband material too. Both are energizing. My whole new life is energizing: a new town, an education, new friends.

Samuel hosts parties with lots of booze at his place in the international student housing complex. This Friday, he's made a Malawian stew and has a twelve-pack of

Coors. I bring a six-pack of Full Sail Amber and homemade cornbread to go with the stew. Isabelle, who comes straight from our office, swung by the store and picked up hummus, pita and a bottle of wine. Patrick brings a pizza, apologizing that he doesn't know how to cook, and a six-pack of beer. Clint brings sausage that he made from elk, which I imagine he killed with his bare hands, and a pint of whiskey. Anne brings a bag of potato chips and a six-pack of beer; not near-beer. Bummers, she must've succumbed to the real stuff. Serves her right for playing with fire like that, an alcoholic drinking near-beer. Wait a minute, I used to drink *no* beer.

The Malawian stew is dark and rich but simple tasting, not spicy. "This should have oxtail in it"—Sameul points at his bowl of stew—"but the store here has none. So, I use beef." He shrugs. "The meat counter man, he looks at me like I am cuckoo when I ask, 'Where is the oxtail, man?'" He chuckles and scoops up a bite of stew with my cornbread. Chewing thoughtfully, looking at the ceiling, he then deems my cornbread delicious, though not as good as his wife's nsima, which he says he eats every day back home.

I've formed a comfortable connection with Samuel, made more comfortable by the fact that he clearly loves his wife. He continues to tease me that I better find a husband and start cranking out some kids. Another part of our connection is based on me recognizing myself in his alcohol consumption, only he is drinking full-on, like I used to, and I am managing my drinking. On a recent field trip, he was so hungover—still reeking of booze from the night before—he vomited just outside the van. He told everyone it was just motion sickness. I felt so much empathy for him. I know of this embarrassment and the necessary lies. There's one surefire way to know when an alcoholic or addict is lying: their lips are moving.

Three hours into tonight's dinner party, Samuel has cranked up Paul Simon's *Graceland* album and is dancing around the place. By the time "Diamonds on the Soles of Her Shoes" plays, he has everyone but Clint dancing. It seems that mountain men don't dance. An hour later, Samuel plays "Homeless" over and over and is slumped on the couch, weepy about how he misses his wife and kids. All the booze is gone by then too. The end to any decent party: no more booze and the host is weeping.

When and wherever I drink, I try to drink like everyone else. When I hang out next door with Sunita, we don't drink. Upstairs at Heather and Eric's, there's very little drinking and always in moderation. I finally try one of Eric's icy gin and tonics with lime, which is more refreshing than I expected. More refreshing than I hoped. A second one would've been even better but I wanted to keep our evening as classy as those cocktails.

The environmental grad students drink more heavily. I gravitate toward Samuel on those nights because he is funny and married and drinks to excess. Next to him, I look sober. Next to him, I can drink several beers, quickly, without being noticed.

I notice, though. I notice the euphoria. Despite my life

actually being pretty good, the alcohol makes everything perfect. A five-beer buzz lets me soar.

The only thing interfering with me drinking like everyone else are all the faces and voices of the people who helped me get sober several years ago. They won't go away. Sometimes, they seem to be right in front of me, still reaching into the inferno to pull me out.

I keep slapping their hands away. *I'm fine.*

The first man I date, post-Scott, is Clint. Based on my husband material research, my gut tells me that he's not a good candidate, but he is gentle and handsome in that grizzly, mountain man way (a little too hairy) and likes to hike. So, we go out for dinners, drinks, a few hikes. We start to fool around some, but I don't let that go too far. I'm not falling back into my old behavior wherein I get tipsy and my clothes fall off with whichever guy I'm so-called dating.

After several dates, I'm pretty sure we're not a good fit. Clint is too ... passive. I don't see him really going after life, full of ambition and dreams. Maybe it's confidence he's lacking, which I can't hold against anyone given my deficit in that area. But Clint compensates for any lack of confidence by being cocky. The saying, doubt is loud, confidence is quiet, applies to him only not in volume. He talks softly enough but mostly about himself.

The bottom line is, I don't think he's the man for me.

Which is another good reason to keep my pants on. This will prevent *me* from feeling guilty and *him* from getting hurt. While I think it considerate of me to spare him the sex, I suspect he doesn't see it that way.

Despite keeping Clint at arm's length, he keeps trying to nudge in closer. After one goodnight kiss, during which I am thinking, I need to break this off, he pulls back for one of those look-deeply-into-my-eyes moments. I try to look back at him, but my eyes flit this way and that, focusing anywhere but deeply into his eyes. That intimacy stuff, letting someone look into your soul, arms wide open and all that, doesn't come to me naturally. If you ask me, that's a perfectly good way to get your heart ripped open.

With his arms wrapped around my waist, Clint is still trying to hold my gaze. Then he cocks his head to the side. "You were hurt or something in the past, weren't you? It's like you can't really let me in. Or won't."

That does it. I look straight into his eyes. You know what I see? I see a man who is going to get crushed by someone, but not by me. I can't take the guilt. Clint embodies the V word—no, not vagina, that word I can handle, having been raised by a nurse—vulnerable. I can't stand the word and despise the condition of vulnerability: defenseless and exposed. Clint is like a character from a romantic movie, in which he and everyone else is wearing their hearts on their sleeves. I don't watch romantic movies.

Apparently, his question about being hurt in my past was not rhetorical because he is still looking at me, waiting. I contemplate telling this passive mountain man about being raped at the end of a sawed-off shotgun by my high school sweetheart, Mark. When I consider telling him this, what comes to mind is the image of Clint saying, Oh, really? What kind of shotgun? I stifle a giggle, making me aware that I am quite tipsy. Telling him about this part of my past might shut him up, but I don't want his pity. I don't want much from him. I need to move on. Besides, I've had about enough of all his tender, emotional crap. The only emotion I have is the desire for another drink.

"Haven't we all been hurt?" I finally reply. "I broke up with my boyfriend back home not that long ago. Guess I'm still ... getting over that." *Uh-oh.* An addict's lips are moving. "I'm probably not ready to get serious. And you're graduating in a few months."

"So, what?" he says, dropping his arms from around my waist. Freedom, at last. I step back.

"I don't want to get involved right before you leave. Me and my ex just went through that. Long-distance relationship ..." I shake my head. "It's better for me if ... we're just friends." My pulse quickens, like it always does when I break up with a guy. Here comes the hypervigilance. *No anger in his eyes. His jaw isn't clinched. Neighbors can hear if I scream. My gun's between my mattress and wall. Front door's closer than the back.*

Clint is watching me, no doubt wondering what the hell is wrong with me. Slow down, I tell myself, everything's okay. Silently, I draw in a big breath, hold it then slowly release it. I look him straight in the eyes. At least, I owe him some eye contact. Plus, crazy people avoid eye contact.

He lets out a long, exasperated sigh. "I really care about you. I like you. But being friends with you isn't gonna work. I want more than that." He watches me, waiting still for something I can't give him, then glances around my apartment. He moves toward the front door.

Back door's best way out now.

With his hand on the doorknob, he pauses. "If you change your mind, let me know. Things don't have to end when I graduate …"

I nod. "And if you want to hang—"

"I won't," he says. "I don't wanna just be friends." He gives a little head shake, in confusion, sadness, disappointment or all the above. Then he leans in and kisses my *cheek*—right out of a romance movie—and walks out.

My wicker loveseat gives a squeaky stretch as I drop onto it. After a few minutes of silence—not in honor of my almost-relationship with Clint, simply waiting for my pulse to return to normal—I crack open another beer.

EIGHT

Greek Mythology

My class has just completed the hardest part of my course: mock debates between the founding fathers of the National Park and Forest Services. Several of my students invite me to join them in celebrating. When we enter My Office tavern, I find the name pretty clever given the blue-collar crowd already drinking there at five p.m. These people are clearly "working" late at the office. Unlike Rico's, My Office has only four beers on tap, none of that fancy microbrew crap for this crowd. Strictly business: Miller, Coors, Budweiser or Pabst Blue Ribbon.

I tell my students what a good job they all did. They carry on about how great Alex was, who keeps waving them away, being very modest. I'm not saying this in front of the group, but Alex truly was the star of the debate, demonstrating a great deal of humor, terrific acting skills and a solid understanding of the course material. He had the class cracking up and, when he finished, breaking into applause.

In addition to being humble and talented, Alex is also very attractive. How unfortunate. He looks a bit Greek, with olive-toned skin, bronzy-brown, wavy hair and a well-trimmed mustache and goatee. I do like a man with a mustache—no choice in that, since my father wore one his entire life.

A couple of hours (and three beers) later, all of my students, except Alex, go looking for a more hip scene. Alex and I stay, enjoying the music *not* blaring from the speakers. These patrons have worked all day, they don't want to boogie.

"I'm showing my age cuz I'm diggin' this music," Alex says, rapping his fingers on the table to Journey's "Wheel in the Sky" song. He grins at me, now bopping his head in time to the music. "Love it."

"Me too. Takes me right back to my teen years, which tells you how old I am."

"Yeah, I'm a little older than most students."

"Hey"—I put my hands up in innocence—"I didn't say anything about *your* age." Though I can't help but smile because I *was* wondering. No way is he in his early twenties, but I don't dare ask. We teachers have to be careful what we say to students.

He looks right at me, smiling too, but his eyes have gone serious. He's also stopped backup drumming for Journey. "You've got the best smile."

Well, that wipes my smile right off *my* face. This is the

first time in my life where being flirty with a man could get me in trouble. What am I saying? Being flirty with men always got me in trouble.

"Listen, Alex, I'm your—"

"No, I'm sorry," he says. "I probably shouldn't say that to my TA." He shakes his head a little. "Even if I'm older than her."

"Oh, I doubt that."

He taps his chest, grinning. "Thirty. I started college late. But I've only got one semester left. Was in the military, then worked some before I figured out what I wanted."

"I get that. Not the military but taking a while to figure things out. A *long* while. I'm almost twenty-seven."

"That's younger than me, and you're in graduate school already. Must've had your shit together."

"Trust me. Took me eight years to get an undergraduate degree."

"What else were you doing?"

Part of me wants to be honest with Alex. He seems a little broken like me. Maybe he had a tough start in life too, or a past drinking problem. He *is* keeping up with me this evening—we're both on our fourth. It might be the beer, or the connection I feel, but I want to open up a little. Maybe we can be friends. I'm allowed to be friends with a student.

"I had a little trouble ... with drugs." I pause for a reaction. Slight raise of his eyebrows, waits for me to say more. This is no slap in the face for him. I like that in a man—I mean, a friend—I mean, a student. "Cocaine. And all that goes with that."

I'm not about to tell him what "all that" entailed or how it culminated with me hiding in the attic with a half-kilo of my father's cocaine, a cop car out back. Telling Alex this could be social suicide. Telling a student this could end my graduate school career.

I glance around the room, then at the bar. "Wanna another beer?"

"Lemme get these. You got the last round."

When he settles back at the table with our beers, he says, "So? What happened?"

"While you were at the bar?" I grin.

"Nice try." He sips his beer. "With you and drugs? If you want to tell me ..."

I take a big swig of courage. "Started young, too young really. Following in my brother's footsteps, I suppose. Ran away from home, spent some time in juvey. My poor mom, she was scared for most of my teen years." I'm sticking with the light version of my life.

"I gave my mom a few scares too. Drinking, mainly." He nods, frowning. "How'd you get straightened out?"

"Basically, my mom did an intervention. Then I went five years not using anything. Didn't even drink."

"Right on!" He bobs his head enthusiastically.

"I only started drinking again when I moved here."

"You mean, like a few months ago?" His brow furrows a little in concern.

"It's fine. I just had a ... rough childhood. When my

parents divorced." How lame—my parents divorced. Whose haven't? "Me and Dad were really close, and he, kind of, disappeared on us ..." Oh, I am done with this dribble. Poor me, poor me, pour me another drink. I take a good pull off my beer.

"You're okay now?"

"Yeah. As long as I stay away from the drugs. And tequila."

He leans back and laughs. "I stick with these too." He taps his beer.

When we head out of the bar, he says, "Hey, I live right up the hill. Wanna come up for dinner?"

I have a nice buzz going, and Alex is easy-going and forthright, like he has nothing to hide. And did I mention, good looking? It could be beer goggles but he looks like a Greek god to me. Zeus is inviting me for dinner. Zeus, *my student*, is inviting me for dinner.

"Thanks, but got two cats at home wondering where their dinner is."

"Maybe some other time?"

I shrug.

"This student-teacher thing's gonna be a problem, isn't it?"

Forthright and bold. I like that in a Greek god. "I don't know. Dinner's okay, I guess."

"Good. Hey, I've had a few too many drinks to drive but lemme walk you home."

He looks so warm and inviting. I envision him saying

GREEK MYTHOLOGY · 59

good-bye on my porch instead of here. No, he'd waltz right through my apartment door and make himself at home. The Siamese would love him, rub against his legs. Rub against my *student's* legs. "That's okay," I say. "I don't live far."

"Are you sure? I'd feel better if—"

"I'm fine." I start walking away, then glance back over my shoulder. He isn't walking the other direction; he is stepping away from me backwards with his eyes on me still. I think Zeus is checking out my ass.

"By the way," I say over my shoulder, "you were great in the debates today."

"So, am I getting an A?"

Now I'm walking backwards. "Depends on what you get on the final." A mischievous, crooked grin peeks out from under his mustache. I turn my back, and my ass, to him and jog across the street.

He yells over to me. "I make a mean steak. And killer bananas foster."

Damn it, Zeus. "You trying to bribe me?"

"Hey, I need all the help I can get."

"Not true, and you know it." I wave good-bye and don't look back.

That week, it's all I can do to keep from smiling when Alex walks into my class. He grins at me every time he asks a question or I look in his direction. In an effort to avoid any favoritism, I practically ignore him. At the end of each class, I busy myself with papers, other students, talking with Don.

After class on Friday, Alex shows up at my office. "Dinner tonight?" he asks.

I shake my head. "I'm in the middle of some research."

"Come on. You gotta eat sometime."

"Can't tonight. I mean ... I'll *eat* tonight, just not at your place."

"I'll bring something to your place."

Luckily, my phone rings. It's Don. Covering the mouthpiece, I whisper to Alex, "It's Dr. McKee. Gotta take this." Then I wave him out of my office.

Next Friday, he's back in my office inviting me for dinner. These Greek gods sure are persistent.

"Okay, but this isn't a date. Just friends."

"Got it." He puts his hands in the air all innocent-like, showing me that he has no weapons. Except for that jaunty smile; that's a weapon.

Alex makes me a terrific steak dinner. And bananas foster is quite delicious: bananas caramelized hot and fast, so they don't get mushy, with butter and brown sugar, then doused with rum and served warm over vanilla ice cream. The sticky-sweet, rummy aroma and taste is almost ... sensuous.

A couple of weeks later, I reciprocate and invite Alex for dinner at my house. As I cook, he sits on the floor, legs stretched out, and lets the cats check him out. Muffin, my fourteen-year-old, settles right down on his lap.

When dinner is ready he says, "Mind if I eat down here?" Stroking Muffin's back, he pleads her case. "She's so comfortable. I can't disturb her." She is sprawled out, legs dangling off his thighs, purring shamelessly. Traitor. We eat dinner next to each other on the floor. What cat lady can resist this?

By the time final exams are turned in, I ask Don, since he's lead faculty for the class I'm teaching, if another graduate student could grade Alex's test.

Don throws his hands in the air in question. "Why? What's the problem?"

I feel my cheeks getting flush. Don is a super smart professor in the research and data realm, but for a social scientist, he doesn't seem to understand people, at least, not women. Ranchers, yes. Loggers, yes. Women, not so much.

"Alex and I have been ... hanging out a little." I'm tip-toeing here, making sure I say nothing to make him question my professionalism and yank that teaching assistantship. "We're just friends, not dating. But it doesn't seem right for me to grade his exam."

"Ohhh." For a few beats, he stares at his desk, or at the mess scattered all over it, maybe contemplating whether he should clear off some of that crap. "How about Isabelle? She TAs my other class. Ask her. If that doesn't work, I'll do it."

Having Don grade Alex's paper would be more unfair than me grading it; Don has a reputation for being a hard-ass on tests. Isabelle agrees to grade his exam but not without first razzing me about hitting on an innocent student. *Yes, so helpless.*

Alex gets 100 percent on his exam, fair and square.

As soon as the semester ends, Alex and I are together most weekends, either at his place or mine, because drinking as much as we do gets expensive at a bar. No longer teacher and innocent student anymore, we're fooling around like a couple of high schoolers, but I say no to sex. High school boys referred to this—foreplay that doesn't lead to the actual play—as a girl who won't "put out" or the more sophisticated "dick tease." But years of sitting on a couch—a therapist's, not the high school fore-play couch—helped me understand that sex is no good if I'm not friends with a guy first. If I can't talk about sex with a man then we shouldn't be having sex. So, I wait and get to know Alex better.

He is undeterred. He must've been one of the nicer high school boys, willing to wait longer than most. One evening, he sips on a beer and plays with the cats while I'm cooking dinner. Out of the blue, he tells me I have a perfect ass. My jaw drops. I turn and stare at him. He makes no attempt to be discreet, he is drinking me in, his eyes roaming up and down my body like he owns it. Now, I know my ass isn't bad—all that hiking—but it definitely isn't perfect. The thing is, he makes me *feel* like I have a perfect ass. He is so carnal. Where some people wear their emotions on their sleeves, Alex wears his libido on his sleeve. Yet, he doesn't pressure me. Patient and sensual is a pretty good combo in a man. Still, I resist.

Another evening, he tells me I'm like a wood nymph.

"A what?" I say.

"You know, like a woodland sprite."

I shake my head. "What's that?"

"They're mythical fairies who live in the forest, flowers and leaves woven into their hair. Huge, inquisitive, green eyes." He locks eyes with me. I don't look away. Unlike with Clint, what Alex wants from me is something I can give. He wants my "yes." Alex is focused and driven, and I know exactly what he's driving at. These pages of my instruction manual are well-worn and dog-eared.

I lean over and kiss him, long enough that he slides his hand to the back of my neck, gently holding me there. The instant I lean back, he releases me.

"You're too much," I say. "How does an ex-military guy, studying forestry, know about mythical creatures?"

He pulls his lower lip over his mustache, sucking in, seemingly, the taste of me left there. "I read a lot. I like mythology. Nymphs are playful and cheerful like you." His gaze drops down to my lips, he runs his thumb across them, parting them. His eyelids grow heavy and his voice gets lower. "And fragile."

Fragile? He thinks I'm fragile, as in frail and weak?

He pulls me up and walk-kisses me over to his couch. By the time I let him take my shirt off, I've stopped analyzing whether I'm fragile and why he thinks so. He releases a little moan when he nuzzles my breast. He kisses down my belly to my jeans, looks up. "Can I take these off?"

Why do I stop a Greek god, who makes heavenly desserts and thinks I am a fairy-thingy with a perfect ass, from unzipping my jeans? Alex makes me feel sexy and beautiful and wanted, but I'm trying to see what's there, if anything, besides that intense physicality. One other tiny, red flag: whenever we're together, we drink. Booze and men were always a dangerous combo. It could be Alex or the beer making me feel this good, and I'm honestly not sure. When I'm straight, he's still a great person but seems overly smitten with me, a titch ... clingy. And now that I'm drinking again, even in moderation, I don't trust my instincts where men are concerned.

So, using my mythical fairy powers, I manage to keep my jeans zipped.

By springtime, I solidify plans to travel to Russia with Janet, a political science PhD student, and one of her advisors, Leslie, who is some kind of public policy expert. I talked with them on a conference call but won't meet them until our flight. We'll be visiting the community where a Chernobyl-model nuclear power plant is located. The plant provides electricity to St. Petersburg and is being run by the same people who ran it last year, under the communist regime. Last year, the plant also had a radiation leak. Recent world political changes that even an ex-junkie like me couldn't have missed—the end of communism in Eastern Europe and the fall of the Soviet Union—make for a tense backdrop for this simmering environmental conflict.

When I tell Mom about my trip, she is excited and a

little worried.

"Is this power plant safe?" she asks, sounding worried. "If it's like Chernobyl, that was a nightmare."

"It's not exploding or pouring out radiation but groups there are protesting against the plant. That's part of what we're exploring, why they're protesting. We're not even going in the plant. Had to get permission just to get in the town." All the sudden, that doesn't sound very reassuring.

"Will you have escorts or ... I don't know ... bodyguards?"

"We'll have hosts, people who work for the city, and a translator. The women I'm going with went before, and they're going back, so it can't be that bad. And the University is putting it all together ..."

"Well, you might start taking kelp tablets." She pauses for several seconds, during which time I wonder what on earth she is talking about. "That's what they gave people after Chernobyl. Keeps your body flush with iodine." This is so completely my mother. The collapse of the Soviet Union. Post-Communist Russia. Political upheaval. Yes, yes, but did you take your kelp? "So your body doesn't take up any radioactive iodine from the air, or the water. Or the food."

"Oh ..." That's a little chilling. Hadn't thought about radiation from last year still being in the food chain, bioaccumulation and all that. "Uh, where do I get this stuff?"

"I'll send you a few bottles."

Haven't I given my poor mother enough to worry about? Booze, drugs and now, radioactive iodine.

NINE

Vodka

G oing to Russia will be the most important, far-reaching thing I've ever done—aside from working as a wilderness ranger—and I want to be taken seriously. I want to wow the Russian team and my American colleagues. To even have a chance, I need to steer clear of any alcohol.

Traveling with two older, professional women to the former Soviet Union is more than a little intimidating, bringing out all my self-doubts. Janet looks to be in her late-thirties, has returned to graduate school after a decade as an attorney. She is all business: dark slacks and a blazer, short-heeled, black pumps, salt-and-pepper (mostly pepper) hair pulled back in a tight, low, business-like ponytail. Very assertive. Leslie is much softer. She is pushing fifty and looks like a former hippie: no make-up, hair graying at the top but still strawberry blond below, loose skirt and billowy-sleeved blouse, clunky jewelry. Very approachable.

The sixteen-hour overnight flight is brutal. For the first hour, Leslie and Janet have in-depth discussions, and Leslie tries to include me, which I appreciate, as I worried they would ignore me or be dismissive. They order rum and Cokes and sip them, all professional-like. I watch them loosen up, laugh more, develop a rummy glow. There isn't much they can do to include me in *that* comradery—it's a members-only club. A rum club.

I could order myself a rum and Coke and join in their glow. No, I'd go for the bourbon, Jack Daniels. Without the Coke. Just ice. Only I'm afraid I'd go for another, then another, and another. Ohhh, the damage I could do in sixteen hours with a handful of those cute bottles. Crammed in the window seat beyond my colleagues, each bottle would be passed right over their heads. They would lose count. They would look at each other on the sly, cock an eyebrow in disbelief. I'm sure Janet has a harsh, judgmental look, and Leslie, a disappointed-mother look, neither of which I plan to see on this trip.

I order tomato juice. A perfectly safe drink because I never have and never will drink a bloody mary. I sip my juice and *don't* think about how much better it would taste with a glurg or two of vodka. *Blech!* I sip my juice and chat as if I belong on this plane, belong on my way to a business trip in the former Soviet Union. I chat like I'm indifferent to their second order of rum and Cokes. No thank you, I tell the flight attendant, no more juice. Who wants more than one bloody cup of tomato juice?

When Leslie and Janet are most of the way through their second drinks—these social drinkers take *forever*—I turn to my papers. With my lips barely parted, unnoticeable, I breathe through my mouth, avoiding tempting whiffs of sharp butterscotchy rum. I study my conversational Russian and re-read documents and articles about nuclear power plants, natural resource conflicts and the situation under the brand new Russian government.

Eventually (and luckily) I conk out and snooze as much as I can in the three-square-foot space between Janet, the side of the plane and the seat in front of me.

We land late the next afternoon, Russia time—I've lost track of what time it is back home—in St. Petersburg, the city that up until last year was called Leningrad after the first Soviet Union Communist leader. Having grown up in mortal fear of the Soviet Union and the United States starting World War III, earth reduced to an apocalyptic, nuclear wasteland by a couple of old guys pushing two red buttons, I can't stop my heart from pounding as I step foot on the tarmac.

The sky is surprisingly bright and sunny and the air cool and damp. There are no soldiers in formation or armed guards alongside the plane, not even airport personnel escorting us into the building. However, I question the judgment of the architect who designed the five glass columns sticking up from the terminal roof that resemble nuclear cooling towers: stout with slightly curved sides and flat tops. Skylights, I trust, to brighten the interior on dark, gray days. They must've been designed before the Chernobyl meltdown.

Leslie, Janet and I head to the restroom to freshen up before going through customs. Leslie stuffs a few tissues in my hand, saying, "You'll need these." I have no idea why she thinks I'm going to cry in there.

The restroom has the musty, sulfur smell of sewer gas and of soured urine teaming with bacteria. Still, nothing to cry about. On the back of the toilet is a stack of four-inch squares of cut up newspaper. What kind of reading material is this, I wonder. As I finish peeing, I notice there isn't any toilet paper, not even an empty toilet paper holder. *Ah,* the newspaper squares and Leslie's tissues! I make a mental note to buy some tissue at the first store we go to.

The sinks have cold water but no soap or towel of any kind, paper or otherwise. Five minutes into my first international trip, and I'm starting to understand how easy I have it in America.

All freshened up, we make it through customs without any problems. Right outside customs, we see a young woman holding a sign with our names. She is our translator, Irina, a very talkative college student, cute in a Dorothy Hamill kind of way, including an identical dark blonde bob haircut.

She leads us outside to an old-looking bus, where an even older-looking driver slings our luggage into the back. We settle in, along with a handful of other bedraggled, weary travelers. As the bus chokes and sputters into motion, Irina tells us, in near-perfect English, about St. Petersburg as the bus rattles past it. She focuses on the city's history and says nothing of the multi-storied, streaked and discolored concrete apartment buildings, mile after mile after mile of them.

When we begin to pass small towns, everywhere there are flimsy, do-it-yourself greenhouses. Irina says anyone with a patch of land grows at least cabbage and potatoes. They have to with the new government because it is very difficult to obtain these food staples.

"Last government provided much of our food, but now we have to buy it." She gives a weak shrug. "Me and my babushka—I live with her—we search for good prices for food every few days from ... I think, in English, it is said 'black market?' These people who buy up supplies then sell at any price they want. Very high prices. They are like criminals." She clicks her tongue and stares out the window for a moment. "But I have opportunities"—she waves her hand in a circle encompassing the four of us—"like this. To translate for Americans was not possible one year ago."

Images from the past few years flash through my mind: President Reagan asking Gorbachev to tear down the Berlin wall; Americans cheering when the wall came down; the first Russian Presidential election. I'm in Russia for thirty minutes, and already I see a completely different view of the world. To be exact, the view from the actual other side of the world.

As much as I want to keep listening and learning, my body has slammed into its own little wall. My eyelids are involuntarily closing, my body floating and swaying with the bus movements. Janet is already zonked out, so, taking her lead, I lean against a window and crash. I'm gone to the world, both sides of it.

The next thing I know, Leslie is shaking my shoulder and saying we're here.

"Here" is a palatial house with wide, stone steps out front and walls made of massive, rough-hewn stone blocks. The mansion is nestled into a grove of trees. Our hosts, Mikhail and Oleg, are waiting for us in a grand entryway.

Mikhail has clearly worked with Janet and Leslie before, greeting them heartily and kissing them on their left then right cheeks. Oleg is more reserved, shaking everyone's hands while a cigarette burns in his free hand. Mikhail is tall and slender, but I can see muscular biceps and pecs pressing against his dress shirt. He must be a weight lifter. From our introductions, with Irina translating, I understand that he works for the Sosnovy Bor administrator, which I gather is the equivalent of a mayor, and Oleg is Mikhail's assistant. Oleg is a short, stout man, a little pudgy around the midriff, and looks only a few years older than me. He talks very little, perhaps because he is a subordinate, or just a quiet man, or because Mikhail never stops talking. Irina tells us we can get settled in our rooms then meet them in the dining hall in an hour.

My upstairs room is modest: a twin-size bed with an ornate, wooden headboard and matching armoire. A tall, narrow window, framed with heavy embroidered curtains, looks out into the trees. Down the hall is a shared bathroom.

Dinner is served family style: two large, round loaves of very dark bread, smartly called black bread, which is hardy and chewy with a subtle tangy, nutty, rye flavor; heaping platters of roasted potatoes, onions and cabbage; canned herring; and a spicy, fried sausage. Mikhail explains how Oleg drove around for an hour to find us good sausage. I'm dismayed to discover that the good sausage has pockets of fat that ooze when cut and gristly bits when chewed. *Why, yes, I love herring!* Comparatively, canned herring on a slab of black bread is a tender chew. Our dinner also makes me keenly aware of how easy my life is in America. I may have had a rough childhood but I never had to search for food, not even the week I, as a teen runaway, survived on bologna, Velveeta and cheap beer. When I could scrounge up the money, that was available at every corner store.

I'm settling into my herring and black bread, rather enjoying the non-gristly, salty-rye combo flavor, when Mikhail says he wants to make a toast.

Fuck.

As soon as the vodka bottle is plunked on the table in front of him and shot glasses are distributed, Mikhail becomes even more animated. Oleg begins to smile and make eye contact. Having Americans here on business is, apparently, an occasion, and I don't want to be disrespectful. This is certainly an occasion for *me* to be here in Russia. Also, I never liked vodka, so there's no harm in one shot.

Mikhail, with his shot glass raised in the air, goes on and on, barely pausing long enough for Irina to translate, then finally says something like, "Za tee-bya!"

Irina says, "To you!" We all lift our glasses and toss back our shots. Instantly, I remember why I never liked vodka: very little flavor and a medicinal burn all the way down to my stomach. With that out of the way, I take another bite of black bread, hoping to stop the burning.

To my dismay, fifteen minutes later, shots are being poured again.

Fuck. Fuck.

Mikhail waxes poetic again, glass in the air, then toasts to something else.

"To our meetings!" Irina translates. We all toss back another shot of bitter medicine. I chase mine with more black bread.

Damn it if, ten minutes later, Oleg doesn't have *his* shot glass in the air and the server comes around to fill our glasses.

Fuck. Fuck. Fuck. I subtly cover my glass with my hand and whisper to the server, "Nyet." I toast with my water glass instead and hope no one notices.

For the next hour, I lose track of how many toasts are made by Oleg and Mikhail. The bread is gone. That bread was my savior, giving me something to busy my mouth and hands with come toast time and, with any luck, sopping up the vodka in my stomach. Discreetly, I continue to limit how many shots I take and even fill my shot glass with water once or twice. Regardless of my efforts, I'm feeling the effects. My brain, the part that is still trying to kill me, is saying, Whoop! Whoop! Bring it on! We're in Russia, drinking Russian vodka. The successful graduate student part of my brain is saying, Get me the hell out of here.

Finally, I lean over to Irina and explain that I've got jet lag, need sleep then excuse myself. I don't stick around for her to translate for the others—they'll probably want to toast me goodnight.

As I lay in bed, my mind is racing. If this toasting happens at every dinner, I'm screwed. Trapped. If I skip the toasts, I might offend our hosts or appear juvenile. Even Irina, who is younger than me, is keeping up. I'm so afraid I'll get drunk and do something or say something stupid, and it's too late to say I don't drink. That's what I should've said. From now on, I'll lift my water glass in the air, and if anyone asks, I'll say I don't drink that often.

Leaving my room for breakfast, I almost bump into a stout woman outside my door. She has a vacuum cleaner in tow and points at my bedroom. "I clean, da?" Her hair is twisted into a bun and her face is full of deep wrinkles that make her look older than I suspect she is. At eight in the morning, she looks tired already.

"Da," I nod. "Pazhalusta." As I step out of her way and she walks past, my nose stings with her body odor. I'm aware that in many countries people don't wear deodorant, and I don't mind the skunky smell of natural perspiration. But this is more than perspiration. She is sweating vodka; her B.O. is combustible. This isn't a hint of alcohol on someone who had a quick nip before work. For her to reek this bad, she must have been pickled the night before. Maybe she's been pickled for years. There is a future in which I could've become a leathered, middle-aged woman, saturated with alcohol at eight in the morning. A horrific thought comes to me: I still *could* become such a woman.

When the cleaning lady comes the next morning, reeking of vodka again, or still, I say, "Nyet, spasibo. Nyet clean." I shake my head. It's not really the alcohol fumes that I can't tolerate, it's the sorrow. It's the wasted life of my alternate future self.

"Nyet?" she asks then says something else in Russian.

"Nyet clean." I pull my door closed behind me and give a little wave of my hands in front of her. "Spasibo." So she doesn't think I'm a stingy, rich American trying to stiff her, I hand her a few one-dollar bills. She smiles widely, exhaling vodka breath like a dragon—I breathe through my mouth to avoid inhaling the flames.

For the rest of the trip, I pay her *not* to clean my room.

Each day we meet with various groups and dignitaries. As I converse with Russian professionals and my American colleagues, and share some of my knowledge, I occasionally feel like a phony. For the most part, I push those If-they-only-knew thoughts out of my mind and press on. This isn't the time to glance back at how far I've come, though I keep reminding myself that I worked hard to be here. I earned this privilege.

When we meet with an environmental group, Janet and Leslie ask me to take the lead, since this is my field. Now, when I could use a shot of courage, there isn't a shot of vodka in sight. Which is a good thing; I would slam it. Anything to take the edge off.

Our meeting is held in Mikhail's office, a windowless room where several women are crowded around a cluster of tables. As far as I can tell, this is a group of concerned citizens, mostly mothers, who talk, with Irina translating, about the local nuclear power plant and radiation leaks. The most notorious leak occurred last year and captured the attention of Greenpeace.

I scribble notes as fast as I can, my hand aching and the rickety table under my pad wobbling. The group tried numerous times to meet with the power plant managers with no success, until Greenpeace got involved.

"What do you want the plant managers to do? To change?" I ask.

They speak to Irina for quite some time, she nods, asks questions, then finally translates.

"They want to know when there is leak so they can take children away for worst part." The thought of a mother leaving this town with children after a known radiation leak, then returning shortly thereafter, is devastating. My mother is worried about me getting radiation poisoning while I'm here for two weeks. "And they want to know how bad is leak," Irina continues.

"Safety," I say to Janet and Leslie, who are sitting on either side of me. "They just want safety."

"And information. Some certainty," Janet adds.

"What happened after the meeting with the managers?" I ask.

More lengthy Russian dialogue, then Irina turns to us. "Plant managers put in ... how do you say ... way to monitor radiation ... ah, radiation machine?"

"A Geiger counter?" I offer.

Irina points at me. "Yes. Now there is sign that shows radiation level each day." Oleg pointed out that sign to us, like one of those digital signs in the US that displays the time and temperature. This one displays radiation levels. In red letters. *Tonight, I'm taking two of Mom's kelp tablets.*

"Did this address their concerns?" I ask.

"I don't understand question," Irina says, shaking her head.

"Is the group satisfied? Are they happy with the Geiger counter?"

There is only a brief exchange in Russian, during which the women let out such a round of tsking and scoffing that I hardly need Irina's translation. "They say radiation number on sign never changes, or changes very little. No one believes it measures radiation. It is ... fake. They are sure."

"What will they do now?"

More translation. "They will keep pushing for change. They want scientist, who does not work at plant, to check for leaks. Possibly scientist from Greenpeace." Something tells me that's never going to happen.

After being in the crowded, windowless office for two hours, the gray, cloudy sky outside seems bright and refreshing. In the not too far distance, I see the white and red tower of the power plant. *Shit! Where's the car?* Always a good place to escape from radiation.

Leslie, Janet, Irina and I say very little on the drive to our next appointment.

We meet with staff from a local newspaper in a run-down concrete and metal building but with windows all around. They tell us the power plant has scientists, but neither the managers or the scientists will say much to the paper. Mainly the good news: how much power is generated, plans for another reactor to come on line. *That's good news?* The managers won't respond to any of the reporters' questions about leaks, the Geiger counter or the data it is supposedly collecting.

On another day, we visit a children's orphanage where all the kids are given kelp tablets daily to prevent thyroid cancer from radiation. At the hospital we visit, the nurses explain that all the patients receive kelp tablets every day they are there.

Hope you can't overdose on kelp tablets, tomorrow, I'm taking three.

Each day, I learn about resource conflicts and nuclear

power and Russia, so much information, it feels like I'm drinking information from a firehose. By the end of the first week, I've filled two notebooks (not with a firehose, just my pen). The conflict with the power plant is fascinating but the situation is very complex. If I were to use this as a case study for my thesis, I'd need to come over here a few times or stay for months. But the risk of radiation exposure over two weeks is worrisome, even with Mom's kelp tablets.

Then there's all the vodka. There's no pill that I know of to reduce the risk of vodka exposure. If there is one, give me a whole bottle!

Wherever we eat dinner, there are vodka bottles and shot glasses. Always. I am heroically trying to toast with my water glass. Not always. From the way my associates are walking gingerly and talking softly some mornings, I know I'm not the only one suffering with a miserable headache, a queasy gut and/or regretting vodka. Every evening, I rail against becoming a pickled, old woman. Every evening, I wage another battle against Russian vodka.

TEN

More Vodka

The night I lose the battle against vodka is, appropriately, in a castle. That night, I raise the white flag, succumb to the fire-breathing dragon, surrender to vodka.

Russians love Hans Christian Andersen fairytales, so much so that they built a children's park in his name. This is no playground with plastic slides and swings. This playground has magnificent bronze sculptures of the Steadfast Tin Soldier and the Little Mermaid, with shiny, bright worn spots where kids climb all over them. The foundation of the park is a small, built-to-scale stone castle with multiple round turrets and a water feature reminiscent of a moat. Mikhail has reserved one of the turrets for our farewell dinner and invited several people we met with over the past two weeks.

In preparation for dinner, Oleg drives Leslie, Irina and I around town visiting shops: nondescript doors in nondescript buildings mysteriously identified by Oleg as places where one can purchase various items. Two weeks ago, when we first went into one of these shops, I'm glad I didn't know how to ask in Russian where the tissue paper was because there was none to speak of. Not one single roll of toilet paper or box of tissues or package of tampons. Today we're searching for the good vodka—really, there's good vodka?—which must be hard to find because we're headed to a third shop.

As I'm wondering about the wisdom of two Americans traipsing into Russian black-market shops in search of vodka, a policeman behind us chirps his siren. Oleg pulls over and walks up to the policeman who is climbing off his motorcycle up ahead. They talk while the three of us in the car watch in silence. Irina appears strangely calm, indifferent. My heart is racing. A cop, in what was the Communist Soviet Union a year ago, just pulled over a car with two Americans who were scouting around for black-market vodka. I don't have a clue if any part of this scenario is illegal, dangerous or could end with us in the Gulag. I don't have a clue if there is still a Russian Gulag. But I'm sure there are Russian jails.

Oleg shakes a cigarette out of his pack and offers it to the cop. *Hmm. Never tried that when I got pulled over.* The strapping man in uniform sucks on his smoke, plucks a piece of tobacco off his tongue, chats with Oleg, tosses his head back in laughter. As if I have nothing else to think of, Dad pops into my mind. Strapping men in police uniforms always draw my attention and remind me of Dad, probably always will, causing a flash of admiration, even adoration. Meanwhile, this policeman has not readied his cuffs or drawn his gun, he simply crushes his cigarette butt on the road with his boot, straddles his motorcycle and pulls away.

Off we go again in search of the good vodka. Oleg never says a word about the incident, and Irina offers no explanation. As far as I know, that policeman just wanted a smoke.

Late that evening, we dine on the second floor of one of the turrets of the Andersengrad Park castle. Inside the castle, most of the outside noise is dampened by the twelve-inch-thick stone walls, and it smells damp, not mildewy, more like a sidewalk after the first rain of the season. With no electricity, the only light is what streams in through five arched windows, but it's bright enough because today is the longest day of the year, the summer solstice. How auspicious, I think. This feels like I *am* entering a fairytale.

We're seated at a long, narrow, rough-hewn wooden table in stiff, straight-backed chairs. The men, and only the men, are toasting everything: us, them, our health, our families, Russia, America, our partnership, Hans Christian Andersen (okay, that one just seems like an excuse to have another drink). This good vodka tastes as medicinal as all the other vodka we've been drinking, but after a few shots, the ones I'm unable to evade, I can't taste a thing.

Overcome by all the people, conversations and trans-lations—Oleg and Leslie discovered they both speak

French, so we now have Russian-English, Russian-French and English-French translation—I start to lose track of my vodka avoidance maneuvers.

Later, I'm drained by the curmudgeon inside me who is *constantly* trying to keep track of and control how much booze passes my lips.

Later still, I'm swept away in the rowdy celebration of our successful trip. The killjoy inside me is worn down and, finally, stops battling the toasts and the vodka and the merriment.

My brain hoots, Yes! Open the castle gates. Drop the planks. Let in the vodka.

Before the sun sets around ten p.m., someone lights fat candles on bronze holders bracketed into the castle walls. Several candles are lit down the middle of the table. This *is* a fairytale. A faint memory starts flickering around the periphery of my thoughts: one of my parents—Dad, I think—read me a tin soldier fairytale when I was young. Maybe the very same Anderson tale upon which this castle was based. All that I can grasp from my hazy memory, from my woolly brain, is the story's end. The tin soldier is thrown into a fire and melts. I'm pretty sure his lady burns alive too. Surely the Russians didn't build a *kids'* park around that story?

A commotion across the table brings my focus back to the room. Leslie is standing, swaying actually, and making very intentional, direct eye contact with everyone around the table. She is radiant, her long hair glowing in the candlelight and her round cheeks rosy from vodka. Oleg and Mikhail are murmuring to each other. I feel a tug of embarrassment, a preemptive cringe, for Leslie, wondering what she is about to do or say. She lifts her shot glass in the air.

Now Mikhail motions for her to sit down. He seems to be trying to spare poor Leslie some humiliation. The other men at the table are muttering and looking slightly flustered and slightly amused. The Russian women look rather tickled.

Janet, Leslie and I, baffled, all look over at Irina, who says flatly, "In Russia, women do not usually toast." She shrugs, bored with the men's mutterings. "It is how it goes. It is fine though. You are guests. You can toast."

Mikhail says something eagerly to Irina, who listens to him, unimpressed. Then, she translates, without any of Mikhail's vigor. "Please. Mikhail would like to offer *you* toast."

Leslie's jaw tightens. Her shot glass isn't overhead anymore but isn't back on the table. "With all due respect," she says, bowing slightly toward Mikhail, "I'd like to offer a toast."

With that, Janet stands too, her shot glass in hand. Leslie's glass goes up again. Mikhail shakes his head, smiling, and gestures for her to continue.

Wow! These women are so brave and powerful. They are leaders, showing me and these Russian women, and the men, showing the world, that things can change. They are making things change. Women can make a damned toast in Russia. In solidarity with Leslie and Janet, I lift up my shot glass, brimming with vodka, and stand with a flourish. A little too much flourish.

Behind me, my heavy chair clatters to the stone floor. I am so mortified. I am so unprofessional. I am so drunk.

In a flash, my brain comes to the rescue. For once. *Who cares? You're still standing. No one even noticed. Besides, a woman is making a toast here.*

Mercifully, Leslie starts to stammer and all eyes move to her. "To our Russian friends and our continued ... friendship. Thank you for your ... friendship." Oh, yeah, she's drunk too. She turns to Oleg and speaks in French, presumably saying the same thing, while Irina translates in Russian. All the women are grinning wildly as everyone, even Mikhail, tosses back the good Russian vodka.

I don't recall picking up my chair or setting it upright but am now sitting in it. I'm disoriented. Something isn't right. I blink, scan the room. Blink. Blink. The row of candles on the table are much shorter, their sides warped and collapsing, wax pooling at the bases. A good amount of time, an hour or more, has passed since Leslie's world changing toast. But I wasn't present for that passage of time.

Ohh, I know this missing time. This is no magic, the stuff of fairytales. This is a blackout.

A spike of fear strikes my chest so hard it seems my chair could fall back again, with me in it this time. *No, no, no, no. I don't do this anymore. I don't drink like this anymore.*

It has been years since I experienced the horrific panic of a blackout, coming to with no recollection whatsoever of what has transpired, if I said or did something inappropriate, something far worse than toasting a room full of men or knocking over a chair. Like in Star Trek, I was teleported out of and back into the castle, except my body never left, only my brain—or soul or whatever disappears during a blackout. My body stayed here in the castle. That I know of. Oh god, maybe my body left too, slipped into an adjacent room with one of the men. *No, no, no.*

Trying to stitch together the black hole, I assess the situation. Leslie and Janet are talking to Oleg and not paying any attention to me. The smokers are clustered at one end of the table with overflowing ashtrays. Mikhail is there having a lively conversation, perhaps a heated one, with the newspaper manager. I'm sitting next to Irina and Sonechka, a nurse from the hospital, who is standing and miming something.

Sonechka looks like she is marching. I have absolutely no idea what we were talking about or what she is demonstrating. Some kind of big conflict? Police marching? The military? She relayed some important information that I have missed.

A shudder runs through my body. I'm chilled to the core. These stone walls have sucked all warmth from me, hopefully not while some man and I were pressed up against a cold, damp window ledge, groping.

Sonechka speaks in broken English. "You know"—she widens her eyes, more adamant marching, some lunging, hands flapping for me to get her meaning—"bunzovsteil, bunzovsteil!"

I look blankly at Irina.

"It is video from America." Irina articulates the words slowly. "Bunz—ov—steil."

"*Ohhh.* Buns—of—steel. Yes, yes, I know the video. Very popular in America."

"Da! Da!" Sonechka says, pointing excitedly at me. We're talking about a damned exercise video. I'm having heart palpitations and cold sweats over an American exercise video. Conversations clearly deteriorated while I was away. "I love veed ... veedyo. I do it ... evrry day." She pats her rump, grinning proudly, then plops her steel buns into the chair next to me.

I continue to engage with Irina and Sonechka, though with far less enthusiasm than Sonechka has for *Buns of Steel,* because I'm fixated on my blackout. Everyone else has been slamming vodka all night, I justify to myself. Maybe *everybody* is here in body only, vodka-saturated bodies, our souls floating around elsewhere. Ghosts in a castle. But I can't go back to living this way. Back to wondering how I got home. Or not going home. Or wondering who I went home with. This fairytale could become a horror story.

When we finally stumble back to our accommodations, the eastern horizon is ever so slightly beginning to brighten. Another familiar, dreadful feeling: panic when I realize I've partied all night and am far too hammered to be at work in a couple of hours. And *this* work is so important, a symbol of my progress, of how far I've come. This is work on which my future success might hinge.

Blackout drinking and all-night partying could blow it all.

Wait just a minute, I reason with myself. Janet, Leslie and the Russian team were right there with me, all night long, and they don't seem fear-stricken. Why should I be? When in Rome ...

Looking up at the sky, in desperation or a prayer-like gesture hardwired from my religious childhood—no choice in that matter since Dad's father was, ironically, a preacher—I'm bewildered to see the Milky Way galaxy staring back down at me, solemnly taking in the world as it has done for millions of years. My cottony brain can't reconcile this mystical sight here in Russia, on the other side of the world from where I've seen it before. I suppose the galaxy would be visible from all over the planet. But when it's almost dawn? Glancing at my watch, I'm shocked to see it's only two a.m.

Of course! White nights. It's not dawn, it's only two. The relief that washes over me is visceral, sending shivers all over my skin. I can still get several hours of sleep before our working breakfast. I'll be well-rested for sight-seeing in St. Petersburg before our flight home. What a glorious, generous gift from the universe. An answered prayer. A most fortunate sign. I'm okay. We're just a few professional women letting loose on a special occasion. Everything is fine.

When I awake, my pounding head is *not* so fine. My eyes are burning. My throat is so parched it hurts to swallow the small amount of spit I manage to pool in my mouth. I'm never drinking vodka again. Never.

In all fairness, our hosts seem to also be in sorry shape because we have a very quiet morning with little talking and no nodding, hugging or cheek pecks. We're all limiting our head movements. Also, an unusually light breakfast is served: soft boiled eggs in dainty, ceramic egg cups, black bread with jam and several pots of strong Russian Caravan tea. The tea is dark and rich, almost smoky tasting, and begins to clear my head. After two cups, I am buzzing with caffeine and sugar. This stuff is better for a hangover than coffee. In a country that consumes as much vodka as Russia, they'd have to have this kind of tea.

We arrive in St. Petersburg with a few hours to kill before heading to the airport. Irina glances at her watch and has a conversation with Mikhail and Oleg, which ends with the three of them nodding all around.

"We can go to Nevsky Monastery," Irina suggests. "It is Russian Orthodox church. Priests will lead mass soon with bells and …" She squints, thinking, shakes her head. "Like singing. In Latin. It is Gregorian—"

"Chanting? Gregorian chanting?" Leslie offers.

"Da. Chanting," she agrees. "Monastery is very old, three hundred years. Many famous people buried in cemetery there. Beautiful buildings, grounds …"

I was expecting the vibrant, twisted onion domes that are so characteristically Russian, but the monastery has more of a European architecture common hundreds of years ago: domed roofs topped with bronzy cupolas, arches and columns everywhere. The buildings, painted rich golds and rusty pinks, sprawl across a compound of well-manicured gardens, dotted with fountains, all smack dab in the middle of bustling St. Petersburg. A serene enclave among the never-ending drone and occasional screech and honk of city traffic.

Irina tells us that, before entering, women must cover their heads. While I rejected organized religion long ago, I have no bitch with any church and don't have a problem showing a little respect at one. So, we walk through the tables outside where people are selling prayer beads, prayer ropes, religious souvenirs and lots and lots of scarves.

I knot my new scarf under my chin and solemnly enter the church. It seems fitting to end my Russian trip with a visit to a church, then a cemetery, because this morning, I felt like dying.

Burning wax and smoke is instantly in my nose and eyes. It is shadowy and murky up in the vaulted ceilings, but down here dozens and dozens of candles are burning. Candlelight is flickering on the stoic priests and on their ornate robes, the heavy gold brocade shimmering. Permeating everything is the chanting of the priests: low and deep and melodic and haunting. Their song—really, it can only be described as a chant—rises and falls, swells and subsides. Sometimes their chant grows soft, softer, a hum, only the vibration of a solitary voice, then silent. Then *all* the priests' voices, deep and resonating. I am entranced.

This ancient ritual is reverberating into my entire being, into my soul. Hopefully, the chanting will clear out some of the muck in there.

When we exit, I squint into the bright day. Surprisingly, my soul does feel a little less wasted, even as—or especially as—we stroll through the cemetery. Things could be worse, right? Many of the plots have a brightly painted, metal table with attached bench. Just enough room for one person to sit and, I suppose, grieve. Irina tells us these tables are for people to pay their respects. She demonstrates tossing back a shot of vodka. Of course.

We make one last stop at a souvenir shop. This place looks suspiciously like a liquor store, with row after row after row of vodka. But so many different varieties. How ever to decide? I wince when I recognize "the good stuff."

I buy four bags of Russian Caravan tea.

ELEVEN

A Drinkingship

The Siamese are ecstatic that I'm home, purring circles around my ankles. Alex practically does the same. He hugs, no, holds me and keeps beaming at me and wants to make me dinner. Exhausted from having flown halfway across the planet, all I want to do is crawl in bed with the cats and sleep for twelve hours. Also, after my Cold War with vodka, Alex looks suspiciously like a vortex of booze swirling around a drain, threatening to suck me down with it.

I've been no victim in our drinking relationship—a drinkingship—I've been a willing drinker and poured plenty of booze into this vortex. But when you see a whirlpool, a swirling eddy in a river, it is often a sign of underlying danger. Another wilderness reminder: if part of the river is being sucked into a whirlpool, stay the hell away. I spent the last two weeks paddling away from the edge of a vortex. I'm defeated and want some distance between me and alcohol, which means putting some distance between me and Alex.

I haven't forgotten my plan to find the recovery groups with all the ol' geezers, the people who will understand me without me having to explain myself, the meetings at which I will feel at home. But I'm swamped and need to get caught up with Don and plans for my thesis. Soon. I'll find those meetings soon.

Don and I talk at length about my Russian trip, and he agrees, it sounds like a fascinating, rich case to study but will take much longer than a year to conduct the necessary research and write a thesis. The travel and the translation and the politics of trying to interview power plant managers are too challenging. Not to mention the vodka, which I don't.

Instead, we start discussing water disputes here in the state and, eventually, I decide to compare two highly visible, contentious water conflicts, one settled by lawsuits and the other using a collaborative effort. The research will involve me interviewing as many of the disputants as I can.

Over the next two weeks, I research both cases and write up a proposal, which my committee approves. I'm eager to get started. I've got a lot to accomplish in the one year I have remaining at the university.

Alex calls to see how things went with my graduate committee, which is so thoughtful of him and so ... intellectual, not his usual orientation. His focus is usually a bit lower than my brain. Not to say that he isn't a smart guy.

But intellectual stimulation simply hasn't been the foundation of our time together. When he hears I got the go-ahead from my committee, he wants to celebrate. That sounds suspiciously like toasting.

I drop my head back, exasperated, and stare at the ceiling. I'm living the graduate school dream here, and Alex and his bananas foster don't fit in that dream. Also, he finished his bachelor's degree and, though he hasn't said as much, I think he's sticking around for me. But I'm not interested in him in that way. He needs to move on. He needs to leave. I need him to leave.

"I'm pretty wiped out today. How about tomorrow? Over here, if that works for you. The kitties miss you."

The phone line is silent for a moment. Possibly he is thinking, The *cats* miss me?

"See you around seven." His voice is expectant, excited. I feel guilty already.

Alex shows up with a piping hot pan of homemade lasagna, Caesar salad, garlic bread and a twelve-pack of Full Sail Amber. This man thinks of everything. But I'm only having one or two of those beers because, for what I plan to say, I want a clear mind.

Two hours and six beers later—doesn't everyone keep track of time with drinks?—I'm drunk. Happy drunk. Full Sail into the wind. I'm going places in this life. I'm going places without Alex.

As I tiptoe into this difficult conversation, he catches onto my meaning immediately and looks as if he is blind-sided, looking at me but staring right past me.

"It's not you, Alex. I'm just not in the place for a relationship. I'm gonna be consumed with my thesis. You need to find a job."

"I'll find one around here."

"You have a forestry degree. There are no forests here."

"I don't mind doing something else until you're done. Then we can—"

"No. I don't want you putting your life on hold for me. I'm not ready to get serious."

"Weren't we already getting serious?"

I hesitate on that one. "I thought we were just … fooling around. Partying. Having a little fun."

"Why does that have to end?"

"Because I need to stop partying. And that's all we do. Seriously. I have to get my shit together."

His strong, Greek-god brow furrows with confusion. "I don't know what drinking has to do with our relationship. If you want to stop drinking, stop."

I'm not sure when he started thinking we have a relationship, but I'm putting an end to that. "If I'm around booze, I'm gonna drink. We drink—we get drunk—every time we're together. Think about it," I press.

"I won't drink around you then."

"It's not just that." Deep inhale. "You want more than friendship … and I don't. I don't want a relationship right now."

Alex shakes his head and starts collecting his lasagna

pan and salad bowl. I help him clean up, making sure to keep a clear run at the front or back door. My gun is in the usual place between my mattress and wall, but getting the hell away from a dangerous man is always preferable to shooting him. Paranoid sounding, I know, but I can't help it. I know Alex isn't a dangerous man, but this fear is all driven involuntarily by my hypervigilant instincts. The problem with these instincts is that they kick my lizard brain into overdrive, and the only responses that damned reptile knows are: fight, flight or freeze. To its credit, my lizard brain *is* only trying to keep me alive. Obviously not the same part of my brain that sucked down those six beers this evening.

Until Alex finally leaves, I remain ready to bolt. Once he leaves, I am worn out. I don't even want another beer. I'm worn out by this so-called break up of our so-called relationship. Worn out by researching and drafting a thesis proposal in two weeks. Worn out by lizards and hypervigilance and beer and men. My cats and I snuggle into bed and sleep. I don't know where that damned reptile went; probably perched somewhere, blinking, watching for any danger.

I slink around campus avoiding Alex, a slinky little reminder of how drinking screws up my thinking around men. I pick the wrong ones or get involved when I shouldn't or, generally, get all mixed up. Take one man, add booze, stir and voilà—a man cocktail. That even sounds sick. A male cocktail—rhymes but sounds worse. No matter how I describe it, men and drinking don't mix.

Rattling around in my head is Samuel's warning about how long it can take to find the right man. At this rate, I don't think I'll ever realize my dream of getting married and having kids. But I'm sure as hell not going to have a relationship based on getting plastered and mauling each other.

After my break up, or whatever it was, with Alex, it's difficult to deny that some of my old behavior is creeping back into my life: the Russian blackout, drunken make-outs, hangover bouts. *Hmm*, the common denominator there seems to be the word "out." Maybe life's umpire is trying to tell me something, like, *She's out!* Only I don't want to be out. I will stick my face right into that umpire's face, so close that he can smell my breath (which hopefully doesn't reek like booze), I will poke him in the chest and scream, I'm safe, you asshole!

For the next few weeks, I don't touch alcohol, not one drop, and don't even so much as *look* at a man. I'll show that damned umpire.

I start contacting people to schedule interviews related to my thesis case studies. These interviews will be with ranchers, farmers, landowners, tribal government and state agency employees who were involved in two long-standing, intractable water conflicts. People's livelihoods, their farms and ranches, were being lost in these conflicts. Fish—the sustenance for many tribal members —were floating, belly up, in warm streams with not enough water. Agencies with regulatory obligations were shutting down irrigation water, then being sued. Every time I dial another number, I expect to be shouted at or hung up on, but everyone is willing to be interviewed.

While getting all these interviews set up, I check in regularly with Don and my other major advisor, Warren. Warren is witty and irreverent, as much as a full-professor can be, and wears a thick, handlebar mustache (without the curlicues). His boisterous laugh, which I can hear down the hall from his office, is contagious. He's a skilled facilitator and mediator, so I go to him with all my questions about conflict. Don and Warren have all kinds of helpful advice, suggestions and support, all offered freely. They're on my side every step of the way yet seem to want nothing in return. They're not even flirting with me. What must they want? To share their knowledge? To help me get an education? To help me have a successful career? I ask you!

My brain, however, is not on my side. The morning before I leave for my first week of interviews, I'm brushing my teeth when the thought of a drink pops into my mind. You deserve to celebrate a little, my brain suggests. Such a mundane little suggestion, like a husband of fifteen years saying, Hey, Hun. Let's catch a movie tonight.

Too busy, I tell my brain. I've got work this week. Serious work. Important work.

By lunchtime, my brain points out that I haven't had a drink in a month. *How about a coupla beers this evening. Cuz you can't drink tomorrow while you're—working.* My brain puts a skeptical emphasis on that last word.

You've got to be kidding, I say to that relentless bitch. I

have to get up at five a.m., drive two hours. Conduct three interviews. I am *not* drinking.

By the end of the day, I'm fully preoccupied with the thought of having a drink. I can't battle this obsession alone. If I go back to my apartment, it's going to be trouble. Flipping through the *Yellow Pages*, I find the phone number for recovery meetings in the area—I really should write this number down somewhere or get a meeting schedule. There is a meeting at seven o'clock, in a different location than the first one that I walked by several months ago. A seed of hope. I stay in my office—the real one, not the tavern—until it's time to leave.

On my way to the meeting, I'm praying—to what or whoever will listen—for old timers to be at the meeting, people with decades clean and sober. Please don't let this be only preppy college kids. I need wise, aged ones who can call me on my B.S.

There are twenty or so men and women, of all ages, sitting around the table. My tension dissipates and my shoulders loosen.

As I drop into a chair, my relief is nudged away by a sense of disappointment. Half-listening to the secretary kick-off the meeting, I try to figure out where my disappointment is coming from. This is exactly the type of group I was hoping to find: diverse, people who are a little more world-weary, even a couple of ol' geezers. Recovery meetings aren't that bad, sometimes they're even fun, hearing the stupid stuff other people do while wasted, the lies we tell ourselves. So, what is my problem? I glance around the room. No one I recognize from my department who could blow my cover. Everyone looks nice enough, some people smile at me. These are my people, people who can help me. These are exactly the people I need.

Did you say *need?* my brain asks, all condescending.

That's why I'm so disappointed. Despite my best efforts to drink normally, I'm back at these meetings. I hate needing these meetings. I hate needing anything.

The secretary asks if there are any newcomers, any one with less than thirty days since their last drink or drug. I'm not introducing myself as new. I haven't had a drink in almost thirty days. Besides, I was in recovery for years. With that thought comes a tidal wave of sadness. My five plus years of sobriety are long gone. But I refuse to be treated like a newcomer, like someone who needs help. I'm not new.

Meanwhile, the trying-to-kill-me part of my brain is having its own little meeting. *You don't need these meetings anymore. Your problem is draft beer. It has more alcohol than the bottled stuff. Just stick with the bottled beer. You'll be fine.*

Bottled, draft, it's all the same, I tell my brain. And, yes, I need these groups to combat the bullshit—and the booze—you keep pouring down my throat.

As people around the table share about their struggles and triumphs to stay sober, my internal meeting continues. *I know what your problem is. It's the microbrews. Definitely stronger than the Coors or Bud you used to drink.*

Nice try, I counter. But I used to drink tequila, not Budweiser.

Right, right. Then that yummy Full Sail should be fine.

Shut. The. Fuck. Up. I'm trying to listen to these people here.

Well, excuuuse me.

Before I leave the meeting, a few women introduce themselves and give me hugs and phone numbers. They have the audacity to suggest I call them if I feel like drinking. Don't they know who I am? For years, *I* was the person giving my number to new women. I don't need these women. I don't want their phone numbers.

Now, there are a few men here whose numbers I'd like. *No, no, no. No men. Don't even think about it. Steady. One foot in front of the other. Right out the door.*

TWELVE

Solar-Powered Love

Back at my apartment, I feel lighter and, I have to admit, less lonely. Luckily, there isn't any booze in my apartment. With my thesis project about to kick into full gear, the stakes are high. I don't want to blow it all, and I know, firsthand, how life can turn on a dime. For better or worse.

Tucking the list of phone numbers between some books on my desk, I promise myself that I won't drink tonight. Or this week. Probably not *never* again but not right now.

For two months, I travel all over the state, interviewing dozens of people who were embroiled in conflicts over who has rights to use the limited amount of water available in the driest part of north central Washington.

Every single time I check into a motel, my brain starts in with, Who would know? You deserve to unwind!

Each night, I tell my brain to leave me alone. At each

hotel, I remind myself that I have an interview at eight a.m. (these ranchers and farmers get up early!), which I won't show up for if I drink tonight. The gamble of drinking, when I have so much to lose, is frightening. When I drink, alcohol determines how my evening, or my next day, unfolds.

This week, I'm interviewing ranchers and irrigators who are in a decades-old conflict, including between two families, over surface versus groundwater rights. When I show up to interview John, who uses surface water for his cattle ranch, he comes onto the porch carrying a rifle. *Holy shit!* His rifle is pointing toward the sky, not me. So, there is that.

I stop and put my hands up, palms in plain sight. I'm not planning on being arrested, it's just an automatic response when you're greeted with a rifle. The universal hand gesture for, Look, I'm unarmed. The dust that my car stirred up from his long gravel driveway is settling. This is right out of a western movie: old man with a thick, gray mustache and cowboy hat; young woman from the city; dust; guns (only mine is just a little .38 Special hidden in my briefcase).

He must've forgotten I was coming. "I'm Lynn. I called last week. We were gonna talk about the water situation."

"Figured it was you. Come on in." He scoops his free arm toward him for me to follow.

Only I'm not going to. I'm in the middle of a huge ranch, no one else for miles, and he's holding a rifle. There is no way in hell I'm going into that house. I start to lower my hands, and my briefcase slumps off my shoulder into the crook of my elbow, moving my revolver further from my reach.

He's staring at me, then his eyes flit to the rifle. "*Ah*, don't worry 'bout this. I always grab it when a car's comin' up the driveway. 'Specially with all this crap goin' on."

I can't figure out how to hightail it out of here, professionally. Say I forgot I had another interview first? It's eight in the morning. Ask if he'll meet me later in town? Tomorrow for lunch?

We're at a standstill, a show-down at the O.K. corral.

Then, like a cherub, a slightly plump, rosy-faced woman wearing an apron—kid you not—appears behind John. With one glance, she assesses the situation. Touching his arm, she says softly, "Go put that thing away!" She ticks her head to the left. He glances at the rifle and gives her a sheepish grin. Then he moves in the direction of her previous head tip. Wow, all that ... talking and without saying a word.

"You must be Lynn," she says. "I'm Betty. Come on in." She also motions me to follow her. "Just made us a little something for breakfast."

Without a rifle no longer in the picture, I finally leave the dusty O.K. corral and enter a well lived in but tidy house.

They seem like a potatoes and bacon fry-up kind of couple, but no, her kitchen swirls with aromas of blueberries and cinnamon and butter, transporting me, as smells will do, right to my grandma's kitchen. John saunters in, without his rifle. Taking one look at the crumbly-topped cake Betty just took out of the oven, blueberries still bubbling around the edges, he pecks her on the cheek and sits down. She scooches plates around the table, each with a big square of steaming cake on it, and John digs in.

The three of us talk for over an hour, me furiously writing notes between bites of cake, which is moist and delicate with an occasional crunchy chopped nut. Who cooks stuff like this before eight in the morning? My mom was always long-gone for work by this time, me scarfing down cold cereal—Fruity Pebbles, if I was lucky. Betty and John talk openly and in detail about the water conflict. They sprinkle into the conversation how they were high school sweethearts and raised three kids on this ranch. Their kids grew up right alongside four cousins, the children of Betty's brother, Keith, whose farm is just down the road. Sunday dinners and holidays and seven cousins running amuck, like kids will do, Betty says, smiling.

As irrigation withdrawals from nearby wells increased, including from Keith's well, the creek started drying up each summer. Ranchers, including John and Betty, were left without enough surface water for their cattle. "High and dry," John says, emphatically. "We were high and dry. Didn't have no choice."

For the past ten years, ranchers have been complaining to the Department of Ecology, which finally ran tests a few years ago and determined groundwater withdrawals for irrigation were drying up the creek. Ecology shut down irrigation to preserve the instream flows in the creek, for fish and cattle. In the West, surface water rights often precede and supersede groundwater rights. The farmers who were irrigating, including Sharon's brother, Keith, filed a lawsuit against the Department of Ecology. The Superior Court overturned Ecology's decision and asked the Pollution Control Hearing Board to review the data. The Hearing Board upheld Ecology's decision. The irrigators petitioned the Washington Supreme Court, which will hear the case sometime this year. Meanwhile, irrigation continues and the creek is dry.

Betty gets a tissue to wipe away her tears. John finishes the story with his arms crossed over his chest, mad about the lack of water and maybe about the water rolling down his wife's cheeks. "There ain't enough water to go around," he says, "Period. But we were waterin' cattle decades 'fore they started irrigatin'. We got rights here."

When I leave, John walks me to the car—this time, without his rifle. "There's a sayin' that describes this whole thing," he says. "Whiskey's for drinkin', and water's for fightin'. Never thought I'd see the day I'd be in court fightin' my own family." He shakes his head. "We didn't have a choice," he repeats. "It was that or lose the cattle. Our ranch. Our house. Everything."

Wanting to stay neutral and, truly, having no answers, I just nod and try to give an understanding look. He looks at me for a couple of seconds then scans his ranch. I can't make out his eyes because they're in the shadow of his hat and the sun is blasting in my eyes, but I can see his deep frown. "Is there anything you can do?" he asks. "You know ... to help us all outta this mess?"

Lowly grad student that I am (*If he only knew about my past* ...), I am stumped. I do want to help people in situations like this. Someday. "I wish I could but ... I'm just trying to learn from *all of you* ... if there's some better way to handle these conflicts."

He lets out a big sigh. "Well, lemme know if you come up with something cuz anything's better 'an what we been through the last few years."

He sticks his hand out, and we shake good-bye. He has the strongest, driest, most calloused hand I ever touched.

As I drive away, all I can see in my rearview mirror is the dust kicked up from my car. I'm sad for them but so energized about the interview material. There must be a better way to resolve disputes like this, somehow working together instead of suing each other, like mediation. If mediation can work for divorces, maybe it can work for conflicts like this. This conflict *was* sort of like a divorce, only with some added scientific complexity. And a lot more spouses.

In between my other interviews that day, John and Betty keep coming to mind. They must have some kind of bond to be together for over forty years and still be so loving and patient and kind with each other, still smiling and touching each other. In the hour and a half I was with them, they pecked, patted, nudged, tapped or swatted each other several times. They seemed so ... in tune with each other and seemed to enjoy pleasing each other. Like

John putting that rifle away without a fuss, and Betty making coffeecake for breakfast. Their connection seemed sweet and uncomplicated and warm, like that coffeecake. Someday, I want a warm coffeecake kind of love.

The next week, I'm at Keith and Sharon's house. If I thought Betty and John were upset about the water issue, these two are despondent. If the Supreme Court doesn't uphold their right to keep irrigating, they plan to retire early, try to sell their house. Only no one wants to buy a three-bedroom house on a farm without any water rights, they say. Their anxiety is palpable. They sit next to each other and hold hands throughout our interview. Keith never mentions his sister, Betty.

My interviews are generating loads of information on water conflicts and, secretly, giving me sneak peeks into people's lives and marriages. Evidently, people in their fifties and sixties in rural Washington didn't get the memo about fifty percent divorce rates because almost everyone I interview has a spouse—*the* spouse, the original one. Being raised by a single mom from the time I was eight, I never saw a marriage up close and personal. Who knew that a marriage weathers over time, each one taking on a unique patina.

Maybe I'm in the wrong field of study because these marriages are almost more fascinating than the water conflicts. I could get a double major: conflict and marriage. *Hey, now that could come in handy ...*

During my second month of field work, I interview participants of a second water dispute. Tensions were also high in this case, with irrigation shut offs and lawsuits—the whole whiskey is for drinking, water is for fighting scene. Before the issues came before a judge, all the participants agreed, instead, to form a collaborative group to try and negotiate a resolution. The group met monthly for two years, ultimately, agreeing to a set of rules for water use that worked for all involved, including the regulatory agencies.

As I interview members of this collaborative group, and learn more about the process, I know this is *exactly* what I want to do for a living. I want to facilitate groups like this and help people build consensus and resolve natural resource disputes, without any lawsuits. I have found my calling. For the first time in my life, except for always dreaming of a family, I picture something tangible in my future, something I can actually achieve. This is it. I am in love. No, not with the hippie husband. I am in love with collaboration.

One of the couples who participated in the collaborative group, Jeanie and Hank, are also in love, with collaboration and each other. They're "old hippies from the 60s"—their words, said with grins and a sparkle in their eyes. I think there was a little weed smoking in their past. Maybe in their present. She has long hair pulled into a thick braid, wears no make-up and is slim and fit. His hair is all one length, tucked behind his ears. He has the muscles of a man who has always been active. Probably chopped the firewood stacked outside and installed the large array of solar panels on their roof.

A year after building their home, which they refer to as a "log cabin," their groundwater well started producing fewer and fewer gallons. The neighbors were having similar problems, especially in the summer months. Several neighbors pooled together the money for a study, which determined the groundwater level was dropping alarmingly low in the summer when nearby commercial wells were pumping at peak rates for crops. If people's wells dried up, the houses would become unlivable.

"We didn't want them to lose their farms," Hank says. "Some of them've been here for three generations."

"They're our friends," Jeanie adds. "Our kids all went to school together. Once lawsuits started flying around"—she waves her hands through the air—"things got bad. Then we formed the group—"

"The collaborative group," he clarifies.

She nods, goes on. "The lawsuits were paused, things got more comfortable. Not completely back to normal, but ..." Squinting, looking for the words, she turns to Hank.

"At least we could talk to them, look each other in the eyes." He nods. "But the collaboration took a lot of time, *lots* of meetings. Still better than a bunch of attorneys—"

"Which we didn't have the money for," she says with a huff.

"Exactly," he says, pointing at her. "That collaborative was the only way we could be involved. Way better than a bunch of attorneys *solving*"—he air quotes the word—"things in a courtroom."

"Hey, I've got a few reports ..." Jeanie hustles out of the room.

"A few?" he hollers after her, smiling and shaking his head. "Wait'll you see this. She's got a file like this." With his hands, he demonstrates a hefty stack. He wasn't kidding.

She lugs in a foot-high stack of documents and folders and, grinning triumphantly, plunks them on the table. "You can have these. They describe everything: who was part of the group, how it worked, what we agreed to."

Before I leave, they give me a tour of their house, talking over each other even more, bubbling over with excitement and pride. This is no log cabin. This is a meticulously built, split-log, solar-powered home. Having only seen houses like this in magazines—I've been interested in solar power for years—it's a dream home. My dream home. Their "cabin" sits at the forest edge where there is a jaw-dropping view of the mountains. A gurgling stream runs through their five-acre property.

Taking me down to the stream, they point to a riffle of whitewater where they sometimes see a black bear catching fish. Since getting up-close-and-personal with a grizzly, I've been mesmerized by bears. If I had a solar-powered home where I could see a bear in my yard ... Wow! That could only be a dream.

We stand there and take in the spectacular view, Hank with his arm over Jeanie's shoulder, her with an arm around his waist. There isn't a strip of space between their bodies.

In my hotel that evening, while I review all the documents that Jeanie insisted, and Hank pleaded, I take, my mind drifts to their marriage. They have this huge, shared passion for their way of life that seems to energize their relationship. I wonder if that energy is what makes them laugh so easily and makes them so connected. Or maybe it's the other way around—their levity and closeness energizes their marriage. Either way, the energy between them was radiant and palpable.

Someday, I want a solar-powered house with bears in my backyard. Someday, I want a solar-powered kind of love.

THIRTEEN

Losing My Religion

T hirty minutes after I get home from my last interview, Heather knocks on my door and invites me to a little get-together with some students from Eric's department. I've been to one of those psychology department "get-togethers." They can drink the students from my department under the table. What does this say about the mental health profession? "There's a guy I want you to meet," she says. "David. He's really cute and funny." If I must have a matchmaker—maybe this is what I needed all along, someone with better judgment than me—she's the one. Heather knows people and what makes them tick.

"Is he a grad student or what?" I ask.

"Yeah. He studies addiction. Works in the same lab with Eric."

Perfect. Me dating a cocaine dealer for lab rats. "*Hmm.* I'm not sure ..."

"Come on. Just meet him. You have a lot in common."

Such a normal thing to get introduced to someone. But if I go, I'll have to avoid all the booze and constantly say, No thanks or I don't drink then explain why not. Or worse, I won't avoid the booze. Then there's this David guy, who may hit on me, so I'll have to avoid that too. Or worse, I won't avoid his advances.

While all of this is running through my head, a tiny butterfly starts quivering in my stomach. *Ohh,* I know this butterfly. Her fluttering isn't about meeting a new guy, it's about the anticipation of having a drink. She is a boozy little butterfly.

"I don't have time—"

"For the party?"

"For dating someone. I'm gonna be swamped analyzing data, doing more research, writing my—"

"David's just as busy. In the middle of his PhD research. I think you'd really like him. He's outdoorsy. Kind of shy."

As Heather coaxes, so does my brain. *Just go to the party. You deserve a little break. Have a little fun.*

For once, I agree. With my brain, that is. I often agree with Heather. "Okay. But I'll drive myself in case you guys want to stay longer. I'm beat."

"Yay!" She does a little excited clapping. So does my brain. The butterfly does a little excited flapping. My own cheerleading squad.

From where I park on the street, the little get-together

sounds well underway. I can hear R.E.M.'s "Losing My Religion" pulsing from a small, unkempt house with a weedy yard, a house that clearly has a new renter every year.

Inside, Eric waves at me and points to the kitchen, where I find Heather chatting with a few women, hollering with them, actually, because the music is so loud. She introduces me to them, then I work my way to the overflowing food table. I squeeze the chips and salsa I brought onto the table and peruse the rest of the food. As I scoop a few things onto a plate, my gaze flits to the counter where there is a row of bottles: wine, Jack Daniels, gin, tequila. My gaze stops right there.

In front of the tequila are two bowls, on with salt and one with lime wedges. My mouth starts, literally, salivating. I swallow. I want to look away, should look away, but I can't. The tequila, salt and lime draw me in like a seductive man checking me out with his bedroom eyes. I am captivated.

"Beer's in the fridge," a woman yells to me, pointing at the fridge. She must assume I'm standing there, plate in hand, staring because I don't see anything I want to drink. On the contrary, I see all that I ever wanted in that triangle of tequila, lime and salt.

Then someone's hand is on my elbow. Heather. Next to her is a tall, slender, handsome man. Well, she just passed the first level of the good matchmaker test. He is clean-shaven with unruly hair and a smile that lights up his whole face. I gather from his smile that he also approves of her matchmaking. Heather introduces us then wanders away. A savvy matchmaker.

David and I get the usuals out of the way, though a bit awkwardly because we're practically screaming over the music. When I begin to nibble on my food—I'm famished —he says, "Wanna go out back and find a place to sit?"

Having just taken a bite, I nod.

He holds up a finger for me to wait, and I notice the half-full beer in his hand. The way he heaps food onto a plate, I gather he is also famished.

Protecting our flimsy paper plates, we weave our way through the crowd. The back patio is a breath of fresh air and space and relative quietness. My ears are ringing. There are only a few clusters of people out here smoking.

We settle on the steps, side-by-side, and eat. David begins scarfing his food down, pushing it onto his fork with his fingers. I wonder when he last ate. When I tap on my chin and tell him he has a little mustard smeared there, he palms it off. I can only hope he forgot to grab a napkin.

Our plates now empty—thankfully, the eating frenzy is over—David is still sipping on the same beer. A social drinker. He is funny and talkative, using robust hand gestures. Good thing he was too busy eating to talk earlier, food stuff would've been flying through the air. Unlike many talkative people, he is also a good listener: nodding, smiling, his eyes never straying. The way he listens so attentively reminds me of Uncle Floyd. David eyes are almost sad-looking, like a puppy dog's. His eyes seem to have seen their share of pain.

After an hour, I've forgotten, mostly, about David's feeding frenzy and am growing interested. He has dyslexia. Bad dyslexia. So bad that he must spend an enormous amount of time reading material for his PhD research. He has to read constantly, like all the time, to keep up. He even brought his books here, he tells me, chuckling. Just in case. Left them in the car though.

This blows me away. Not that his books are in the car, though that is amusing; it blows me away that someone with dyslexia can get a PhD in experimental psychology. Talk about never giving up. I'm honored that he is so open with me about his brokenness, yet he doesn't strike me as being vulnerable—*phew!* He is far too self-possessed to be sensitive about something like dyslexia, though he says he was teased mercilessly in school. The little bastards.

"Hey," David says, "I'm gonna get another beer. Want one?" I was so lost in our conversation that I forgot all about the tequila trifecta.

This would be a good time to tell him about *my* brokenness. He does study addiction. I could tell him that I haven't used drugs for several years, that I haven't touched a drop of alcohol for months. If I tell him though, that door to alcohol becomes harder to open. Then, if I want to drink later, I have to get tricky. Heather doesn't even know about my past struggles, so why tell a man who I just met? Besides, I deserve one drink after months of interviews and research and studying. I deserve one drink after months without a drop.

"Sure, I'll have a beer." That seems more lady-like than what my brain is hollering: Bring me back that damn bottle of tequila, will ya? With some lime and salt. Bring yourself a shot glass too, honey.

Having a beer in my hand again after three months is distracting. *Sip it, don't chug it. Don't have a second one. Go ahead, have another. Wait half an hour first. Blah, blah, blah.* The usual. Like wondering if I should have another cookie when I haven't even taken a bite of the first one.

David seems unaware of my altered state of mind, so I must be doing a good job of faking. I'm annoyed that I can't get lost in our conversation again and keep trying to get back into that space where I forget about myself and am in the moment. It's pointless. Evidently, I am unable to be in the moment and have a drink in my hand at the same time.

If David only knew what his lab rats go through as soon as they get into the cage with the cocaine.

Frustrated and unwilling to explain to David about my (or a lab rat's) obnoxious brain, I finish my beer, exchange phone numbers and say good-night.

On my drive home, I'm preoccupied with the fact that I drank only one beer, especially given my brain's persistence. My brain is a radio station that broadcasts 24/7, always on air—KFCK. *K-Fuck radio, for your listening pleasure.* But if I can go a few months without drinking, then have only one beer, I must not have a problem. That three-month break must have reset my body. I can probably drink normally. Now, if I could only find the volume knob for K-Fuck radio.

I'm also a bit preoccupied with David. He is smart and polite (eating habits aside), funny and kind, and so very real. He's also pumped up about his research, which was stimulating. The closest I've come to someone like this was Scott but he was at the end of his school learning, about to embark on his career. Launching a career as a psychologist and starting graduate school are very different life phases. But David and I are in the same life stage, pushing against the edge of knowledge in our fields, geeking out over the potential to make a unique contribution.

A week after the party, David and I go out for dinner and talk for three hours, non-stop, about our studies, our professors, the classes we teach, previous jobs. We don't go much further back than that, which is a relief; tonight, I don't want to skirt around my childhood and my father and my drug abuse.

Our relationship begins slowly and with a heavy focus on studying and analyzing data. This new angle on a relationship is strange, as in foreign, but refreshing. We take turns making dinner and eat and study and talk. David regularly talks with a mouthful of food, so I emphasize the eat and study scenario, followed by talk and study. Eating and talking is overrated. On weekends, we do something with Eric and Heather or go hiking or catch a movie. Dating, I believe this is called. We never go to bars.

Analyzing all my interview data and writing my thesis is overwhelming and exhausting and I love every minute. I'm on fire for research and writing and conflict resolution, for resolving conflicts without lawsuits. I'm on fire for saving the planet *and* the people.

I spend many hours with Don and Warren digesting all my data. When I come to them confounded about how to interpret some data, Don will direct me to research papers to review or to experts I should contact or to Warren. Warren is inclined to say, Great questions, Lynn. Let's go get some coffee and talk about it. To which I'll say, smiling, Come on, just tell me. I know you have the answer. That'll get a belly laugh from Warren, then he'll say, C'mon, let's get some coffee and figure this out. I'll be glancing at the clock thinking how I don't have the time. Then over coffee, Warren will ask me open-ended questions and get me thinking and digging deeper until, finally, things start to make sense.

This must be what advising graduate students is all about: not spoon-feeding the answers to students but making them discover the answers. That, or professors simply don't have all the answers—how could they? Maybe being smart isn't having all the answers but knowing where to find them. In any case, I'm getting skilled at finding answers.

David is a great help to me because he's been analyzing data for years, even publish a scientific research paper already—related to rats, not people, but still relevant. Just look at how much I have in common with those lab rats, at least where cocaine is concerned.

As David and I grow closer, our studying and hiking and eating is interspersed with fooling around. But I stick to my rule of getting to know him before we have sex, otherwise it won't be much fun. No trust, no fun—what a concept.

During the several weeks that I'm waiting to have—I mean, getting to know David, he never consumes alcohol. This is fine, since I'm intentionally not drinking, partly because he isn't and we spend a lot of time together, and partly because my life feels precious. I have so much in the balance and don't want to risk tipping the scales. Alcohol has a way of tipping the scales.

Then late one Sunday afternoon after studying for hours at David's place, he pulls a beer out of his fridge and offers me one. I'm stunned. *Where did that thing come from?* I blink and stare at the bottle. A dry lump forms in my throat. I swallow. Blink again. The balancing scales and the risks are nowhere to be seen. On this lazy afternoon, life is stable, not precarious or particularly precious. Life is normal. This relationship is normal. Drinking is normal.

Flap, flap, flap, goes the butterfly.

FOURTEEN

Lab Rats

The second I touch that cold glass bottle, taste the heady beer flavor and feel the gentle fizz in my throat, I am transported. David is still there on the couch next to me, his warm arm draped over my shoulder, chatting, but what is he saying? Great question, only I don't have a clue and don't care because my brain is back in the kitchen trying to peer into the fridge to see if there's more beer. Since my brain isn't capable of prying open the refrigerator door, it is pestering me like a toddler whose mom has been on the phone too long. If my brain could, it would tug on my shirt, pull my arm, stomp its gelatinous, little feet. My brain would glare at me and poke, poke, poke a slippery, gray finger at the fridge.

Unsettled, I set my beer on the coffee table and lean back, way back, out of the beer's reach. Wait, I'm in charge here. I lean back so the *beer* is out of *my* reach, prop my feet up and turn my attention to David. Only he isn't talking anymore, he is looking at me with his head tilted in that curious, puppy-like way.

"You okay?" he asks.

"Huh? Yeah, I'm fine ... Why?"

"I don't know. You seem a little ... far away."

Ohhh, the fridge isn't that far away. Pursing my lips, all serious like, I shake my head. "Nope. I'm right here." I give his thigh a reassuring rub.

"Good. I like having you right here. Close to me." He brushes his lips across mine, ever so softly, almost a tickle, and a shiver shoots straight down my body. Who knew gentle could be so sexy? Then he gives me a lingering kiss, his tongue soft in my mouth.

Giving him my full attention, refusing to acknowledge my brain or my beer, I say, "I can get closer." Without hesitation, he presses against me, his kisses becoming less gentle, more wet.

"Let's go to my bedroom. You know ..." He pauses for a kiss. "In case my roommate comes home."

"Is that"—kiss—"the only"—another kiss—"reason?"

"*Mmm-huh.* Don't wanna disgrace you."

Seriously? This man is worried about my reputation?

Little late for that, my brain taunts.

No, I remind myself, clean slate and all that. Ignoring my brain's opinion of my reputation, my past reputation, I'm touched that David finds me worthy of such respect. In fact, his respect takes me right over the edge. I can't wait any longer. We're good enough friends. We've been hanging out for *six weeks*—but who's counting? Six weeks is a perfectly respectable amount of time to wait for sex. Besides, my body is screaming for his body.

"I have another reason to your bedroom," I purr into his ear.

His hand was roaming, gently exploring my body, and instantly stops. Right on my ass. He pulls back from me a little. Makes eye contact. "Why? You getting sleepy?" He grins.

"*Ah!*" I swat his shoulder. Wasting no more time, we stumble back to his bedroom, grinning and groping.

There is something wonderful about laughing with a person you're about to have sex with. Real laughter, not drunken or stoned howling. I can count on one hand the men with whom I've been this relaxed and emotionally intimate—*blech,* another mushy word. No question about it though, sex is great when you have ... let's just call it a connection. How can you enjoy sex when you're worrying about how you're performing in the sack or sucking in your gut so you look thinner?

The next day, I'm glowing with contentment and connection whenever I think of David. Whenever I think about the beer I didn't finish, my contentment sours. By the time we came out of David's bedroom last night, my beer was warm and flat, which never stopped me from finishing one before. But I have no doubt watching me chug a warm beer would set off a few warning bells for David. Surely, he's watched his cocaine-addicted lab rats do the equivalent of polishing off a tepid, flat beer, whatever that would be. Oh, scarily, I know what that would be: scurrying around their cage floor frantically sniffing and rooting for cocaine. Good thing I didn't suck down that beer. Good thing I'm going to a noon recovery meeting.

At eleven-thirty, David shows up at my office, also glowing. He doesn't even try to keep that whole cat-who-swallowed-a-canary look off his face. Closing the door behind him, he envelops me in a hug. "I had to see you. Let's go get some lunch." When I hesitate, he adds, "Or just a quick walk."

As much as I want to be with him, I need that meeting. Now. Last night's beer is still calling to me. Any beer is calling—warm, flat, cold, bubbly. I can feel it in my gut, a jittery tension. Like when your boss calls you to his office. You don't want to go because you have no clue if you're getting fired or getting a raise, but you must go. Alcohol is my boss this morning, and I'm pretty sure I'm not getting a raise.

"I'd love to, but I gotta grade papers," I say apologetically. Disappointed face from David. This man wears no masks. And here I am, lying to him about going to a recovery meeting. But I don't plan to go to these regularly or have them be a part of my life again. Once I figure out how to manage alcohol, or stay the hell away from it, I'll put all this behind me. The meetings are temporary. They're hardly worth mentioning.

I pull David against me, craving contact—full contact. "Can you come over this evening? Stay the night?" I rub my hands up his back.

Happiness all over his face and his lips all over mine. Getting lost in him, I think about having a quickie right here on my desk. If we're quiet ... Nah. No condom. And Isabelle might show up. And the meeting. Nudging him away is almost painful. From the desire in his eyes, he also feels the pain.

"When should I come over?" His voice is gruff with arousal.

"Five too early?"

"Now's not too early. But I can wait 'til five. If I have to."

I glance at the clock. It's a fifteen-minute walk to the meeting; I'm going to be late.

"Now get outta here"—I mock shove him out the door —"so I can focus."

After he is out of sight down the hall, I hurry out. This is so screwed up. I'm not hiding my drinking; I'm hiding my recovery. From a man who studies addiction. *This is nuts. I just lied to my boyfriend.* I don't have time to get it all straight. All I have time for is a meeting.

The way that bottle of beer took over last night has shaken me enough that I speak up in the meeting. As I talk about the effect of one stupid bottle of beer, a bottle I didn't even finish, there are nods and chuckles around the room. Then one lady shares about her mental obsession with alcohol. Yes, I think, I *was* obsessed with that beer. Others talk about not acting on their thoughts about drinking, even if just for one hour, or one minute, because the thoughts will eventually pass. Right, just like I *didn't* drink that beer last night. They say just don't pick up a drink or drug, no matter what you're thinking or feeling. Don't pick up, no matter what.

The last man who speaks is wearing a grease-stained, dark blue jumpsuit with a service station logo and his name stitched on the front. Slow and quiet, staring at the coffee cup his hands are wrapped around, he says, "I been in battles before. In Nam. We never went into a battle alone." His brows are furrowed, his eyes scrunched—in pain or sadness, maybe horror. Then he looks me square in the eyes. "And I don't battle this addiction thing alone either. Booze and drugs'll win. Every time. If you're an addict, they'll beat ya every time."

Remembering my battle against vodka in that dank Russian castle, I conjure an image of me flailing around in a suit of armor with a sword, raised shot glasses encircling me. I didn't have a chance. Not in the Russian castle, surrounded by vodka and drinkers and not one single ally. In Russia, I was without any support or defense. But here, I'm not alone. Here at home, I've got a chance.

That evening, David and I devour dinner, then each other. As we're snuggled up in bed, I'm drained. With my cheek resting on his shoulder, I can hear his heart beating. Or is that mine, the way you can hear your own pulse when your ear is pressed against something. Being so close that I can't distinguish our heartbeats kind of blows my mind, in a freaky way. Do I want my heart all mingled up with another's? Not really. Being that close is great when things are good, but when things get bad, as they always do, it sucks. Then you're gutted and your heart is wasted.

This gets me pondering what that guy in the meeting said about battling drugs and alcohol alone. Maybe with David, I can stop being so alone. As if he read my mind, he nuzzles into my hair, takes a deep breath, inhaling my scent, I think. He releases a little, *Mmm,* as if he finds me delicious smelling.

How sexy to have someone love the way your body smells; it's so primal and base. Though I have to admit, I don't love David's smell. I wonder if you can fall in love with a person if you don't love the way they smell. Of course, I haven't enjoyed the aroma of most of the men I dated. Scott was so clean he had no scent, even when we were working out. Once in a while, I caught a whiff his facial cleanser (maybe that's why his skin was flawless). Mark—definitely didn't like his odor. I could detect the anger in his perspiration, the pungency of adrenaline-fueled sweat. There was a charming, smooth-talking man I had a fling with in college. He played baseball in high school, a very clean-cut, all-American kind of boy who taught me about the Orion constellation and bright yellow warblers and about throwing heat. This is, apparently, the term for pitching a fastball, and he described throwing heat with such vigor and enthusiasm that it turned me into a puddle of heat. Never have I been able to watch a pitcher throw heat the same way again. Nonetheless, Mr. Baseball had a delicious, almost musky scent. Ironically, near the end of our fling, he confessed that, when we first started fooling around, he wasn't that drawn to my smell. Damned primal instincts.

"You get all your papers graded?" David asks sleepily. Stereotypical gender typing right there: the woman is thinking about human bonding and connection and primal olfactory reactions, and the man is thinking about work. At least he's thinking about *my* work—progress for humanity.

I should tell him the truth. What will he do, get mad that I went to a recovery meeting? Get mad because I have a history of addiction? No ... get mad because I lied. Deciding to let our heartbeats mingle in peace, I tell him, Yes, I graded all my papers.

As soon as the words come out of my mouth, I understand that lying to someone's face when you're all mingled up with them is messed up. A huge, red flag. Cold-blooded. This realization begins darting around the edges of my consciousness, droning like a blood-thirsty mosquito. *Go away!* This cold-blooded lie won't go away. It is proof that I'm not fully connecting, not letting down my guard. I may not be wielding a sword, but I'm still wearing a suit of armor.

My father is also this way, to a fault. He can, and did, walk away from anyone, including me, without feeling a thing. *Ouch! Damned mosquito!* I don't want to turn out like Dad.

Propping myself up and unmingling a bit from David, I say, "Hey, I was wondering, does any of your research look at recovery from addiction?"

"Like, how the brain recovers after drug use cessation?"

"Umm ... more ... what makes it easier or harder for addicts to recover ... to get off drugs. Or alcohol."

He sits up, excited. "I look a lot at neurochemistry, mainly dopamine—you know what that is?"

"No, what?"

"It's a chemical in our brains. When something makes you feel good, dopamine is what makes you want to do it again." He does a little Groucho Marx eyebrow wiggle and runs his hand up my thigh. "With addicts, it makes them want to keep getting high. Even if there are negative consequences."

Ohh, yes. I know this dopamine.

"It affects tolerance and withdrawal, cravings for cocaine," he continues.

Ohh, yes. I know cocaine cravings.

Trying to circle us back to the real world, to my world, I say, "Does that play a part in relapse?"

He nods. "Definitely. Dopamine kind of wires the brain to want more. Why d'you ask?"

I clear my throat, which has gone tight and dry. "I had a little problem ... with drugs. But it was a long-time ago." There, I said it.

His brows knot up with concern. "Why didn't you tell me?"

"It was *so* long ago. When I was a teenager. I don't usually talk about it." I shrug. "Makes people uncomfortable ... they don't know what to say. I don't really want people to know."

"Did you go to treatment or what?"

"No, just went to counseling. And recovery meetings. You know, twelve-step groups."

He nods.

I swallow. Here goes. "I still go to meetings sometimes, like when I get a craving." There, it's all out. I won't have to lie. What a relief. I smile. He doesn't smile back. "Or a pulse of dopamine," I say, to lighten things up.

Still no smile. "Glad you told me."

"So you can use me as a lab rat?"

"Yes. I'm gonna shave your scalp back here"—he rubs the back of my head—"put in a little probe and a PICC line." He gently pokes one spot on my scalp. "Right here." I bet he's this tender with his rats; those must be the luckiest lab rats around. "Seriously, I'm glad you told me. Makes me respect you even more."

This man! He is too kind. Too kind for his own good.

FIFTEEN

Wilderness Love

By mid-April, I've drafted my thesis with plans to revise and defend it in May, then graduate in June. After I turn in my draft thesis to Don and Warren, David and I take off for a three-day backpacking trip to celebrate.

This is the first time I've backpacked with a boyfriend, and I'm giddy with excitement, giddy to share my love of the wild. It's early in the season, so we can't make it to an alpine lake, always my favorite, because those trails are still buried under several feet of snow. Instead, we head into Hells Canyon—the deepest river gorge in North America, deeper even than the Grand Canyon.

On our descent, a one-thousand-foot drop in elevation over several miles, we take our time, goof off, have a lazy lunch in a meadow and take pictures of flowers and mountain peaks but mostly of each other. For the next two nights, we sleep under an almost full moon, which makes the Milky Way less visible but radiates a pale luminosity over the landscape, a smoldering, romantic setting for the first (and second) time I have wilderness sex. I'm in wilderness heaven. Until the hike out.

We quickly realize this might be called Hells Canyon because it is complete hell to hike out of this steep-walled canyon. I get into my regular uphill groove: don't look back much, slow and steady trudge, sip water regularly even if I'm not thirsty. David is in the lead, me in the back, because I have much more experience backpacking. Another wilderness lesson: slowest person in the front, always, so they don't get left behind. As we climb up, up and up, David becomes quiet, but I'm not talking much either. It's an unrelenting uphill hike. Then he begins to hike slow, slow, slower. His pace is becoming a serious concern because we're not getting out of this canyon before dinner time at this rate. We didn't pack a third dinner.

The sun is casting shadows directly underneath us, our shadows the shortest they've been, so it must be around noon when I suggest we stop for a lunch break.

David only nods, plodding over to a downed log in the shade and dropping his pack, literally—releasing the buckles and letting it flop to the ground. "I'm not hungry, but you go ahead. I'm just gonna rest." When he turns to sit on the log, I notice his cheeks are very red. I would expect him to be flush with all of our exertion, we've been hiking uphill for about three hours, but his skin is flaming.

My wilderness training kicks into gear. He's wearing a

sun hat, so it's not sunburn. It's not hot enough out here for heat stroke. Maybe with the exertion, it's heat exhaustion.

I shift my pack off and lean it against a tree. "You feeling alright?"

His head is in his hands, elbows on his knees. "No, I don't feel so good. Splitting headache." We're not at a high enough elevation for altitude sickness.

I touch his forehead, which is cool and dry, very dry. I glance at his t-shirt. No sweat rings under his arms. My shirt is soaked. "How much water have you been drinking?"

"Um ... not sure. Think I drank most of one of my bottles ..." His voice trails off. I pull both his water bottles out of his pack. One is more than half empty, so he drank at least twenty ounces. Can't be dehydrated.

Maybe it's just overexertion. "Do you have cramps or pain? Nausea?"

"Not really. My legs feel like rubber. Think it's just ... too much. The constant uphill climb, with all the weight."

He looks thrashed, as if he has zero energy, which doesn't bode well for the next several miles. There is no way I can drag him out of here. I could keep pushing and nudging him onward, leaning into his back, but not for hours.

I drape his head with a wet bandana, elevate his feet and encourage him to eat a handful of salty-sweet trail mix until he feels strong enough to move on.

Needless to say, it is a brutally long hike out with stops

every twenty to thirty minutes. By the time we reach the car, we're out of food and water and it's dark. The moon hasn't risen yet. At least I get one more glance at the starry sky.

On the drive home, David rattles on about his heat exhaustion or overexertion or whatever it was, as if it was no big deal, saying, Next time we'll just go day hiking and, Guess I'm not much of a backpacker.

Really? I didn't notice.

Our conversation has me all over the place emotionally. I'm discouraged because David should've been more aware of, or forthcoming about, his backpacking abilities. Maybe he wanted to please or impress me, but he seems oblivious to what a scary situation he put us in. I'm disappointed in him and the last part of our trip. Disappointment in a man is hard for me to let go of because this feeling has a long, fat taproot leading right back to my father. I'm dismayed that David glibly minimizes our backpacking future. Sure, day hiking is fun—in and out of the mountains in one day—but it doesn't get you to high-elevation alpine lakes or to the base of cloud-hidden mountain peaks or to the Milky Way. Mostly, I'm disheartened at this huge, red flag and my shallow reaction.

I'm not sure I can have a long-term relationship with a man who can't backpack. I need a wilderness kind of love.

♡

Ten days after turning in my draft thesis, Don calls me into his office. I expect some direction on a few parts of my thesis that need to be improved. When I sit down, Don's shamble of a desk between us, he leans back in his chair, which releases a loud squeak. He extends his arms, elbows on the arm rests, my thesis in one hand and a pen in the other. "Lynn, this is a valiant first effort."

He could've pushed me over in my chair, and that would've been less of a knock-down. Valiant? As in heroic? What kind of description is that for a draft thesis? I'm a good writer, have even been tutoring other students at the campus writing lab. My face must look stricken because Don smiles. For close to two years, he has been nothing but approachable and supportive, but suddenly his smile seems menacing. With his coffee-stained front teeth all the exact same length —a straight, sharp bite—his smile reminds me of The Joker's smile. The maniacal one played by Jack Nicholson.

Sometimes my mind plays tricks on me when a person who I think I know says something that catches me off guard, especially if they're in a position to do me harm. I think I see darkness or evil in their face, mainly in their eyes, sometimes their smiles, as in The Joker here. It's my instincts going haywire, a PTSD misfiring that, no doubt, stems from my psycho high school sweetie whose behavior could flip like a switch. I try to ignore this misinformation because it makes me feel like one of the patients at the hospital where I worked—the paranoid ones.

When I tune back into reality, Don, who I remind

myself is *not* The Joker, is still talking. "It's well-written, and I agree with your conclusions but ... you have to lay it out more systematically. Or your committee will tear it apart."

"Tear it apart? Why?"

"Social research always gets criticized by the quantitative scientists, for starters. But we can handle that."

"Handle it? You mean, in my thesis or when I defend it?"

"Both. I'm not sending you into the wolves when you defend. I'll be there, supporting you. But you need to write up the social research methodologies you considered, why you chose the ones you did, the qualitative analyses you conducted. The quantitative faculty will have an easier time supporting your research if it's well-grounded in science, even social science."

Qualitative *analyses?* Plural? I've snapped out of my shock and am scribbling frantically.

"And since this is such a new field, you might want to skip conclusions and just have a findings section. Maybe make some recommendations for future research. I've written it all down." He reaches over his chaotic desk and hands me my draft thesis, which, apparently, is also in shambles.

I flip through it, glancing at all his handwritten comments and notes. They're scribbled on almost every single page. "When? When do you want another draft?"

"Depends on how long you think it will take. Your

writing is terrific, that's not the problem. Just restructure it, add a section or two, beef up some sections."

"It'll take months. Most of the summer."

Still holding his pen, he massages his chin in contemplation, back and forth, back and forth. "Why don't you outline the revisions you plan to make in each section, like an annotated outline, and I'll comment on the outline. Just to make sure you're on the right track before you start in on any big revisions."

"That would be great. I can have an outline done in a week but ... I'm not gonna make it for graduating in June."

"No, but you can defend this summer. We'll find a date when your committee's all here. It'll all work out. This happens sometimes with a master's. Takes a little longer than two years."

No big deal then. Sheesh! I need a drink.

SIXTEEN

The Brain and the Butterfly

On my walk home, I'm completely whacked out. I'm shocked and reeling about Don's feedback. I thought I'd written a strong thesis, but why did I think I could draft and defend it in two months? And why didn't Don warn me. Surely, he knew or suspected my thesis wouldn't be finished after one draft. I'm not *that* good of a student. Why would he do this to me? And my last paycheck comes at the end of May, which he also knows. I'll have to extend my lease through the summer but have no idea how to pay the rent.

Maybe I could get some help from Floyd, but I hate to ask. No way am I asking Mom for money; I'm trying to be a self-supporting adult. Dad? Now there is a great idea: contact my previously, maybe currently, drug smuggling father and ask for some money. Great idea!

My body is on autopilot—feet moving, legs lifting, knees bending, arms swinging—but the pilot, big brain up there, is checked out. As luck would have it, my body seems to be aimed toward my apartment, not a bar.

At home, I greet the Siamese, then start pacing. Had I known how much nervous pacing I'd do in graduate school, I would've looked for a longer apartment. But I'm not one to sit and ponder, that lets my mind take over and, before you know it, I'll be browbeaten by my brain. No, I need to keep moving. The girls' heads are moving back and forth, following my path with their crystalline, blue eyes. They have come to think of this as some kind of entertainment: the *Mom is Crazy* game. First one to get bored and look away loses.

I should call Logan, talking to him always strips things down to what's important, to what really matters. But I doubt he wants to listen to me complain about a luxury problem like finishing graduate school. I could call David. He knows all about graduate advisors and committees since he got his master's before he came out here. Glancing at the clock, I know he'll still be in the department's basement (the perfect place to dole out cocaine to rats). Besides, there's nothing to talk about. I have to get a job. That's all there is to it. I'll go downtown, get a newspaper and start looking. I stop pacing. In that very instant, the butterfly comes to life in my gut, and I'm pretty sure it's not all aflutter about finding a job.

There are newspaper stands here and there along the main street. The first one I come to is, of course, a block from Rico's. From this newspaper stand, I can see the Rico's Pub sign hanging above the entrance. Inserting my coins, I pull out a paper and tuck it under my arm. David's place is in the opposite direction from Rico's, but it's only three-thirty; he won't be home for another hour and a half.

Pop into Rico's for a pint, scan the "Jobs" section then go to David's. It's early. Rico's will be nice and quiet. The butterfly is exuberant about this bravo plan the brain has come up with. The two are in cahoots.

Back home to the right. Rico's to the left. *Eeny, meeny, miny, moe.* Too bad there's no twelve-step meeting right now, I think. *Catch a tiger by the toe.* What does that rhyme even mean? *If he hollers, let him go …* What a stupid way to make a choice.

I turn left. For *one* pint. One. That's all the time it will take to review the help wanted ads.

Four hours and several beers later and out of money, I stumble home, full of bravado about Don and his "valiant first effort" talk. Methodology this, methodology that, I think. How'm I gonna finish a thesis with a full-time job? Fuck this.

As I turn onto my street, I see the silhouette of someone moving about on my porch. When I get closer, there's no mistake. That isn't one of my neighbors, Sunita, Heather, or Eric on our shared porch. David is pacing across the porch.

It's funny how old, entrenched behavior, even if you haven't practiced it for years, is hardwired and can automatically jump to life. Quirky behaviors like, say, duping people. Well, I've got a deep groove in my brain for pulling the wool over people's eyes. Could be inherited; thank you, Dad. While I'm not proud of this trait, I know I have it and that it blindsides me sometimes, kicking in when least expected and/or when completely unnecessary.

In the ninety seconds between identifying David and entering my apartment with him, I transform from a drunken woman who has been slamming her problems away, beer after beer, into an only tipsy, disgruntled grad student.

His eyes are wide and concerned instead of their usual puppy-dog appearance. "Where've you been?" He snaps.

"Why you drillin' me?" I can feel the slur in my speech and try to articulate more clearly. "I had a shitty day. Really shitty."

"I'm not drilling you. I was worried about you." His face twists up with confusion.

"Y'don't need to worry about me. I don't need a watch dog." Especially one who can't even backpack, I think.

"I'm not being a watch-dog. When you weren't here at five"—*Shit! I forgot he was coming over*—"I waited for half an hour then went back home and called your office. Called your apartment like every fifteen minutes. Came back to see if you were inside unconscious or ..." My hard-wiring for deceit must be a little rusty because I feel guilty. Feeling guilty, or feeling anything, is not a key element of tricking people.

Wrapping my arms around David's neck—his arms stay at his sides—I say, "I'm *so* sorry. I forgot you were coming." Standing on my tiptoes, I reach up and kiss him.

He doesn't lean down or kiss me back. "I had this crappy meeting with Don. He wants me to redo my thesis. I'm gonna have to get a job this summer. So, I went down to grab a paper, then to Rico's for a coupla beers while I looked at the help wanteds. Probably left right before you got here." For the most part, this scenario is true, and all good hoodwinking has a foundation or at least a kernel of truth.

He lets out a sigh and stares at me for a few beats. Then he leans down and hugs me back, murmuring into my neck, "I thought you were hurt or ... in some kind of trouble."

My body goes rigid with a bright, hot anger. The last thing I need is a man trying to rescue me or, worse, out searching for me. Once he gets me figured out, I won't be hard to find. And he won't like what he finds. Disappointment. A scary girlfriend. A liar.

David loosens his grip on me, and I take a stiff step back. In the space between us, my deception is glaring. My deception is right there, on David's now relaxed face, in his forgiving smile, in his wide-open heart. If David knew how much I drank at Rico's tonight, knew that I am trashed and still able to walk and talk, then he'd have something to worry about. If he knew how much cocaine I was smoking a few years ago, knew that his most addicted lab rats pale in comparison, he'd really have something to worry about.

David has no clue who I am, no clue about the train barreling down the tracks.

He tips his head and moves in so close that I can feel his warmth on my lips right before he kisses me. Then his lips, soft and moist, coax my mouth open. His desire is immediate. In fact, it is pressing against my thigh. A little moan slips out of my mouth and then something inside me breaks loose. It's probably that train.

In a frenzy, I kiss him, my hands on the back of his head pulling his lips hard against mine. His hands are wild over my body, then he pulls off my shirt and unzips my jeans. As I clumsily kick and step out of my jeans and underwear, he takes off his shirt.

We drop onto my bed, and David is inside of me with a relieved moan. Then, he pauses and looks at me.

Oh, please don't ruin this with some crap about love, I think.

"Condom?" he mutters.

Phew! "It's okay. I won't get pregnant." I try to pull him closer.

He resists. "You're not ovulating?" David may not know *when* I ovulated, but at least he understands the power of one teensy, almost microscopic human egg. I like that in a scientist.

"It's fine," I say. Still, he resists, impressively. Damned scientist, I think. Of course, he needs data. "My period will start any day. Like tomorrow."

More slowly, he starts moving inside me, probably calculating risks, but in no time, we're at it again. When he begins to groan, he looks at me, trying to lock eyes. I close mine. I clutch him to me with my arms and my legs and my mouth. Just not with my eyes. Trying to get even closer, I grow wild underneath him. Then, to my surprise, I also climax.

Drunken sex, when I can remember it, is usually dulled and numbed, rarely culminating in an orgasm. At least not one for me.

David's voice is muffled in the pillow next to my head. "*Whew!* What was that?"

"I don't know," I say, spent and releasing a drowsy chuckle, "but it was great."

He flops onto his back, staring at the ceiling with an arm crossed above his head. "That was the most intense sex I ever had."

It was intense, despite me being loaded. I'm perplexed about what unleashed me. Maybe it was David's concern for my whereabouts. No, that just pissed me off. Maybe I was redirecting my anger. Or maybe it's just old, hard-wired behavior, my natural duping abilities springing to life.

Uh-oh. Is that a train I hear?

Out of the corner of my eye, I glimpse David's profile and can tell he is relaxed and content. His heart is wide-open and all is well. All *I* feel is a visceral desire to bolt, like a deer who caught the scent of a bear. I want to get the hell away from my valiant thesis and the call I must make to Mom and Floyd telling them, No, I won't be graduating in June. I want to run away from the terrifying girlfriend that I truly am, the woman crouched inside me waiting for this mushy crap with David to end so she can get back to the festivities.

The only thing I don't want to escape from right now is alcohol. I'm tired of scrambling away from it, always trying to manage what I drink or how many or where. I want to succumb to alcohol, to have at it with booze, full bore, head-on, complete abandon. Unleash the monster.

David, naturally, wants to stay the night. My most-intense-sex bliss dissipated along with my buzz, and my stone-cold heart snaps closed. I need another beer. Or three. And nothing, not even great sex, will stop me.

I used the last of my money at Rico's, drained my meager checking account down to five dollars. I do, however, have a credit card, which Mom co-signed. She receives statements too, so knows when and where I use it and always asks if I need help paying it off. But buying a six-pack at the grocery store will simply show the store's name on the statement. Just groceries.

But I have a bigger problem, more unsurmountable than having no money: how to remove an open-hearted, sex-drunk lover from my bed. Rolling my head over to glance at the clock, the butterfly is excited to see that it's only nine. She starts a little flurry in my belly.

I got this one, says the brain to the butterfly and, presumably, to me, although lately my incorrigible brain has been zipping right past my thoughts or needs or opinions. There are a variety of tactics for this delicate procedure, continues my brain, some work better than others and some are more kind. Unfortunately, you can't have it both ways.

Who let this tiger out of its cage?

The first option, my expert brain suggests, is to break up. *That'll take hours, I snap.* You could start a fight. *Nah, I'm too relaxed.* You could tell him you need some time alone. *That* is *true ... hmm, clever.*

Yes, the last one, encourages the brain. Try that one.

Flap, flap, flap, goes the butterfly.

"Hey sleepyhead," I say, all casual. "You better get outta here before you conk out."

"You want me to leave?" He lifts up to peer over at the clock. "Now?" He drops back onto the bed and gives me a dreamy smile, blissfully unaware of the train coming his way.

"I'm not gonna be able to sleep until I figure something out with my thesis. I want to take a closer look at Don's comments, do a little work on it ..."

"Lemme help." He rolls over, propped on his elbow, cheek resting on his hand. "We can brainstorm things. Sketch out your revisions." Man, is he energized by research.

"Uh, I, kind of, want some down time."

"That's alright. I've got plenty of stuff to read too. I'll go get my—"

"Alone. Some down time alone. If you don't mind." I grimace.

He sits up in bed, looking incredulous—he really should work on some masks. I sit up too. We both sit there not saying anything. I could try brutal honesty and ask if he wants to have a few beers, except I've never seen him drink more than two, and I feel a six-pack coming on. I want to drink away my misery. Then tomorrow morning, I'll start looking for a job.

"Is that okay?" I give him an apologetic smile.

"Not really. I mean, we just made love"—*Eww*, the absolute worst of the unspeakable words—"don't you wanna snuggle?"

That must be what normal couples do.

"I've got too much on my mind, getting a job and cramming through a thesis revision. You know how this stuff takes over." Rubbing my temples, I say, "I just need to focus on it a little, then maybe I'll be able to get some sleep."

Sulking, he begins to get dressed, taking his sweet, resentful time. I glance again at the clock. Nine-fifteen. Plenty of time.

SEVENTEEN

Unqualified

Alone at last with my twelve-pack—seemed a waste to use a credit card for a five dollar six-pack—I don't wallow in my misery. No, I chug the first couple of beers, reconstituting my earlier buzz. After two more beers, things are looking up. After the sixth beer, I'll land an awesome job tomorrow, with part-time hours and high wages. Some beers later (I lose track), I'll be cranking through my thesis in no time, everything is great, couldn't be better.

In the morning, I awaken to an urgent cramping, followed immediately by my mouth flooding with saliva as I race to the toilet. As I'm heaving, I promise to never drink that much again. I'm not sure who I'm promising because the porcelain god I'm kneeling in front of couldn't care less.

Neither can my brain. *Yeahhh. Heard all this before.* If my head didn't hurt so bad, I'd smack that gray blob right upside its head. The butterfly is nowhere to be found, probably tucked away somewhere with her wings flat against each other, sleeping it off.

Sweaty and panting, my head still hanging in the toilet bowl in case I'm not finished, I wrack my brain to recall how many beers I drank. Six, no, seven at Rico's. Then six here that I can remember, but that was hours after Rico's. Twelve or so, depending on how many are left in the fridge. Regardless, too many. Especially since I haven't been drinking that much lately. Lower tolerance. Serves me right for cutting down.

Running a cool shower, I step carefully over the tub and lean against the shower wall, not trusting my wobbly legs. My brain is throbbing against my skull, each pulse excruciating. Behind my eyelids, my eyes are dry and stinging. My mouth is pasty with bile. Slumping down into the bathtub where it's safer—can't get any lower—I wrap my arms around my knees, close my eyes and let the warm water wash over my head and back for a long, long time. A full-emersion baptism after kneeling in front of the toilet; this was a drinking episode of biblical proportions. I stay collapsed there in the tub, moving only to turn the hot water knob up as the water cools, then to turn the shower off when I've drained the tank of all hot water. I, too, am drained. Empty. Nothing but coldness left inside. I'm a dark star, collapsing.

To my surprise, there are five beers remaining in my fridge. So, I drank fourteen yesterday. My very next thought is, Good, some for this afternoon. *What the fuck is wrong with you?* Staring at those beers, I'm stumped about what to do with them. I'm not throwing them out, that's good money down the drain. If they stay in there, I'll drink them.

Closing the fridge, blocking out the beer and the dilemma they present, I rest my forehead on the door. The metal is hard and cold. "*Ahhh,* that feels so good," I mutter. I roll my right temple to the coolness, now my left temple. I'm sure the cats are wondering why I'm rolling my face across the fridge.

The phone rings, the sound mercilessly jarring my brain. Serves it right, that stupid brain of mine. This has to be David calling; Mom calls on Sundays and Floyd would still be at work. I contemplate letting it ring but don't want him showing up here again looking for me. And the shrill, *Brrrnng, brrrnng, brrrnng* is grating on my already frayed nerves.

Scattered all over the desk and floor are pages of my draft thesis—that must've been some party last night. I scooch aside all the paper to unbury the phone.

"There you are," David says cheerily. "I called your office but didn't get an answer. You feeling better?"

Worse than ever. "Much better. What are you up to?" Pressing the phone to my ear with my shoulder, I shuffle through my thesis, putting the pages in order and finding, to my relief, no missing pages though some have illegible or incomprehensible scribbles. Excellent progress made last night.

"I'm in the lab working with the rats." Those lucky

rodents; what I wouldn't do for some cocaine this morning. "Wanna meet for lunch?"

I won't be able to eat for hours. What time is it? Shit, it's ten-thirty. "No, I've gotta get to the computer lab and work on my revisions. I made a lot of notes and edits last night but took the morning off, looking for a job—"

"Find anything?"

"Nothing. A newspaper delivery person," I say, indignant. "Think I'm qualified to deliver papers?"

He clicks his tongue. "Definitely not. Maybe if you got some training first. Why don't you ask your advisor?"

"For what, a job?"

"If he's got some money for you."

"I can just ask for more money? And he'll hand it over?"

"There's no guarantee, but sometimes faculty can drum up extra money. What d'you need, like a few thousand bucks? You can finish your thesis this summer, right?"

"I think so. It's really the methodology section I need to rework. Then tie that in with my analysis and findings."

"Oh, is *that* all?" He chuckles. "Well, you *are* his student. He kind of has to ... or *should* help you finish. Looks better for getting tenure if his grad students actually graduate."

Of course! Don can't let me fail, leave me out here blowing in the wind. It's worth a shot to ask him; better than delivering newspapers.

In the heavy pause at the end of our conversation, I

sense David's reluctance to hang up, sense he is waiting for me to invite him over. And he probably senses that I'm being distant and weird. Horrible person who I am, I don't mention getting together tonight.

On the way to my office, I stop by the newspaper and fill out an application. At least delivering papers will get some cash rolling in. Next, I stop by Don's office and ask if he or the department might have a little funding that would let me to focus on my thesis for the summer. Otherwise, I'll have to get a job. As those words come out of my mouth, they sound like a lame threat: Give me some money or I'll ... I'll ... go get a job.

Since Don responds with his Jack Nicholson's Joker smile, he is either being insensitive, doesn't give a shit or thinks *I'm* joking. Systematically, using clear, if-then logic, I elaborate on my predicament. If TA money ends this month, then I can't pay rent. If I'm homeless, then I can't finish my thesis. If I get a full-time job, then I also can't finish my thesis. Not in a few months.

That little walk-through wipes The Joker smile right off. Don says he'll see what he can scrape up.

While waiting for Don to find some scraps, I stay super busy, too busy to see David more than a couple of times. Every day, including weekends, I'm either in the computer lab, the library or my office (the real one, not the tavern). Some days, all three. Progress on my revisions is slower than I expected. Most evenings, I get back to my apartment late, feed the cats and crash.

Once, I use my credit card for a twelve-pack of "groceries," the cheap kind: Coors. Desperate times call for desperate measures. Combined with the five beers that were left in my fridge, I make the beer last two weeks. That is, two days drinking six beers each, and one day drinking only five beers, all over a two-week period. I also use my credit card to buy some food after scanning and calculating how far I can stretch various items, eventually skipping Velveeta and bologna and settling on dried beans, rice, canned tomatoes and some marked-down ground beef. Really moving up in the world.

I apply for more jobs, one at a coffee shop and one at a bar. The brain and the butterfly think working at a bar is a splendid idea; they're all aflutter. No one calls me in for an interview, not even the newspaper. Apparently, I don't have the qualifications to toss papers onto porches.

Three days after my rent is due, after I've lied to my landlord that I'm waiting for a check to come in, Don informs me that a colleague, William Roberts, a professor in Oregon, is interested in my research.

"What do you mean? Like he wants to review my thesis or something?"

"It means he's got some funding to support your research. Three thousand dollars."

My vision gets a little blurry, and I blink a few times, not wanting to well up in front of my disheveled professor who probably can't handle tears, even ones of joy and relief. "*Ohh,* you have no idea how relieved I am. This is such good new. Thank you *so* much."

He smiles. "You can thank William when you get a chance. It's his money."

"Definitely. What else do I need to do?"

"Nothing. He'll transfer the funds to the department, then we'll keep paying you your TA salary. It is customary, since he's paying for part of your research, to put his name on your thesis. And make him a co-author when you publish."

"Publish what?"

"Your thesis."

"You mean, when it gets put in the library here at the university?"

He leans back and chuckles, like a parent who finds his kid's naivety cute, chuckles hard enough that I catch a whiff of his coffee breath, like bitter, burnt toast. "Published in a journal. A peer-reviewed journal." I stare at him, having no clue what he is talking about. It must have to do with this other professor and his money. Don continues, "It's great research. In a growing field like environmental dispute resolution, you won't have any trouble finding a journal."

"When ... would I do that and ... how?"

"It's not any extra work. You submit a condensed version of your final thesis. Shorten it to fit the journal's requirements." He waves my concerns away. "Don't worry about it. We'll work on it after you defend."

When I said he had no idea how relieved I was to get this extra money, it seems Don, literally, had *no* idea. He has no idea how very far I've come—from the streets of

Columbus and the juvenile detention center—only to run out of money and almost peter out. No idea how close I was to not getting my master's degree after years of classes. Now, two whole minutes after solving my money problems, he moves on to a quick little tweak of my thesis before I publish it.

Totally, Doctor McKee! I'm right there with you. This man is going to drive me to drink.

Instead, I go to my other advisor's office to share the good funding news and the not-so-good, need-to-publish news. I've come to trust Warren and can talk to him about university stuff, even about Don, and I know he'll hold it in confidence. He is a question-authority type of person so a good one for second opinions.

Warren's door is open, but I rap on it. "Hey, you got a minute?"

"For you, more than a minute. Have a seat." Warren always sounds happy to see me and has not once asked me to come back later.

"Got some good news. A faculty from Oregon, Doctor Roberts—"

"I know William. Forest economist. Does a lot of research on collaboration."

"That's him. He's going to contribute or ... give me enough money to finish my thesis."

He slaps his hand on the desk. "That's great news. Congratulations."

"I know. I was out there looking for a job."

"Whoa, a job," he says, grinning. "Let's not get carried away here."

"Seriously. I wasn't gonna be able to pay rent."

"Then this *is* really good news."

"Don said I should put Doctor Roberts' name on my thesis, which I don't mind. But then he started talking about putting his name on my paper when I *publish* it. Like in a journal. He never said anything about publishing before ... Am I supposed to publish my thesis? Do I have to?"

Like all good mediators, Warren is listening attentively, waiting for me to finish. His lips are pursed in concentration and his fingers a steeple under his bushy mustache. When I finally stop blathering, he points at himself, questioning if it's his turn.

I nod.

"First, the name thing's no big deal. Every thesis and dissertation has a slew of professors' names listed after the student's name. About publishing, this is *your* research. And it's good stuff. Important knowledge to share. But, if you don't want to publish it, don't." He shrugs. "Nothing says you have to. And don't let anyone tell you otherwise." He raises his voice at the bit there at the end, sounding indignant, like a crusader against injustice.

"Do most grad students try to publish their thesis?"

"Absolutely," he says, without skipping beat, then grins.

I squint at him, trying to figure out if he's teasing or serious.

He chuckles. "Why don't you just focus on getting your thesis defended, then we can talk about whether you publish it later? You don't have to decide today. Just do one thing at a time."

Of course. I know how to do that. A steady trudge. One foot in front of the other.

EIGHTEEN

Reruns

As soon as I get that paycheck, I pay my overdue rent, go shopping (for real groceries) then, without a second thought—hell, without *any* thought—head straight to My Office (the tavern, not the real one). I'm in a festive mood and want a little pat on the back before I get down to business on my thesis. My Office is the perfect place: they don't have my favorite Full Sail beer, and I won't run into peers or anyone who knows David, which would require me to make up some story when he says, Hey, Babe, so-and-so saw you at Rico's. Why didn't you tell me you were going out? I would've come. My Office is a place where I can celebrate in peace. Unfortunately, in a blue-collar, working person's bar like this, the only "peace" the men are looking for is a piece of ass. I leave after ninety minutes and two come-ons.

It's safer and cheaper to celebrate at home.

Throughout the summer, I congratulate myself with a

few drinks, or more, whenever I complete a milestone: finishing the annotated outline of my thesis revision, Don and Warren agreeing my methodology section is done, getting my weekly paychecks. This milestone drinking requires that I get imaginative in order to slip away from David so I can drink—I mean, celebrate. This creativity is hard work, so I have to bring out the big guns: lies of omission, little white lies and big, flat-out lies.

In my defense, I do feel guilty for all my creativity. Despite David's sloppy eating and his inability to backpack, I enjoy his company, his warmth and his easy-going nature. I admire how he's overcoming dyslexia. If I could share the depths of my struggles, it might be bonding. Although, there's no contest between dyslexia and addiction; I win that one, hands down ... or lose it. If you're more screwed up than someone else, are you the winner or the loser? Irrelevant. I'm the loser in this relationship, hands down. Besides, having a liquid gala with each achievement that moves me closer to a master's degree isn't exactly overcoming a limitation nor is it something David would admire.

No matter how much I want to show him the real me, to let it all hang out, the real me is consumed with all this congratulatory drinking.

David deserves better than this, far better than me. He deserves to be turned loose. So, I'm pumping the brakes. Not hard enough to lay rubber on the road or slam us into the dashboard but hard enough that David probably feels the dig of the seatbelt against his collarbone.

Our relationship skids to a stop the day Don and Warren approve my thesis and tell me to start preparing to defend it before my full committee. It's also a payday. This is a major accomplishment—the revision, not the paycheck—the biggest hurdle remaining to get my master's degree, the crest of the mountain.

I head home earlier than usual, around one p.m., and am minding my own congratulatory business when, a few hours and several beers later, there is a rapping on my door. A stab of fear zaps out from my heart to my limbs. *Jeezus!* What a buzzkill.

My first instinct is to hide. In my addiction-riddled youth, I wasn't above hunkering down in my apartment when I was high and someone knocked. Of course, back then, illegal substances were also being concealed. At least, I know the current knocking isn't the police; nothing illegal here. Still, I want to hide.

Dashing into the bathroom, I think, Can't be Heather. Would've heard her climbing the stairs if she came home. I check my reflection, run a brush through my hair, check my breath. Alcohol. Lots of it. Oh, well. *Knock, knock, knock.* Sunita at four in the afternoon? Nah, she's usually on campus until dinner time.

Heading for the door, I holler, "Coming." That leaves David, but why would he be here this early? Who is taking care of the crackhead rats?

"It's me." David's voice through the door stops me in my tracks. I'm simply not up for being a fraud. I am drunk, the best kind of drunk—joyous, exuberant drunk—and want to stay this way. I don't want to pretend to be straight. I don't want to be a liar and feel shitty about myself. Enough already. Truth be told, I couldn't fool him if I had to; I'm on my seventh beer. There's no choice. I have to end this, to end us, and spare him any further agony.

When I unlock the door, David strolls right in without waiting for an invite or a welcoming gesture. This must be what normal couples do. The more at home he feels, the harder it will be to push him back out the door, to push him out of my life. This is going to suck.

"Hey, what're you doin' here?" I don't even try to articulate clearly; to hell with him if he doesn't like my slurred speech. "It's like, middl'a the day."

He leans down and kisses me. "I stopped by your office to see how things went, you know, with your profs. Your office mate—Isabelle?—told me you left a few hours ago." He shrugs. "I was pretty much done with the rats ..." He has a chipper, optimistic smile on his face. This is going to really suck. His eyebrows shoot up. "Sooo, how'd it go?"

"Great! They loved it." I grab my beer off the table and take a big swig. "Tol' me to get ready to defend it."

"I knew you'd nail it!" He sits down at the table and ticks his chin at my beer. "Celebrating already?"

"Yep." I take another long pull from the bottle, then tip it in his direction. "Want one?"

He gives a quick head shake, and the tiniest of creases forms right between his droopyish, puppy-dog brows. "You alright? You seem kind of ..."

There is one more tactic for removing a persistent lover from your bed, or your house, or your life. This is almost surefire if the lover is a relatively healthy person with decent self-esteem and you're an addict or have some other cagey, secretive or socially-deplorable behavior. Unfortunately, this simple yet effective approach can seldom be used in a kind manner: unveil who you truly are; flaunt your true colors in all their vibrant, blazing, shocking glory; if you must, make a scene.

"I seem kinda what?" I widen my eyes in challenge to his pending accusation. "Huh? Kinda drunk? Think I'm drunk?"

David's smile went straight already, flat-lined, but now the corners of his mouth turn down. The heartbeat of his joy is beyond dead, without a pulse. "You do look ... and sound a little ... intoxicated. Maybe you should slow down."

Tell me how to drink, will you? I'll show you. In a few big gulps, I polish of my beer, which was half-full. Then I burp. Very dainty. "Intox'cated? Yes," I say, giggling and pointing my empty bottle at him. For emphasis, I wag the bottle at him with each syllable. "I'm in—tox—i—cat —ed."

He looks stunned, but I don't care because I'm congratulating myself, damn it, and he is being a killjoy.

"Shoulda seen me when I was younger. Member I tol' you I had a *big* problem? When I was a teenager?"

He looks torn, like he wants to listen to me but doesn't want to hear what I'm saying. "You said you had a problem with drugs," he says quietly. "Not sure you said it was a huge problem."

What the fuck? Is there such a thing as a small problem with drugs? Haven't those lab rats taught him anything? "Well, it was a *big* problem. *Bad.* Runaway. Arrested. Juvenile 'tention center. Drug-dealer boyfriend." I swing my arm overhead, as if that captures the arc of my addiction.

Not wanting to see his bewildered face, I stumble into the kitchen and pop the cap off another beer. "Sure y'don't want one?"

"I'm positive. Listen, I think I should go." He pauses, no doubt waiting for me to change his mind, to ask him not to leave. "Or do you want me to stay?"

"Y'don't need to stay. I'll jus' call you t'morrow."

He stands and hesitates. There it is: the disappointment that I was, inevitably, going to see in David's eyes. "I'll call you later and make sure you're alright."

"Okey, dokey." I open the door and, with a grand sweep of my hand—the one not holding a beer—gesture for him to exit.

Instead of following my grand gesture, he comes in for a hug. He wraps me in his arms, his strong, safe arms, and holds me against his chest. He is warm. My resolve weakens. My arms dangle. Suddenly, I'm exhausted. I want to let the beer slip from my hand and crash to the floor. I want to close my eyes and fall asleep against his warm chest.

But morning will come, as it always does. Tomorrow,

David will be the same endearing, unguarded man, and I'll be the same two-faced bitch.

Stepping away from him, I take a sip of my beer. This allows me to further distance myself: beer up, eyes up, elbow out. Walls up. Who knew you could build a wall with booze? Turns out, it makes one of the strongest walls around because booze makes me unreachable—it makes nothing matter. When my elbow comes down, he is still watching me.

"Are you sure you don't want me to stay?" He runs his hands up and down my arms, a caring, shoulder-to-elbow rub, maybe trying to rub some sense into me.

"Pos'tive." I swat his offer away like it is an annoying, persistent housefly. "I'm fine. Bye-bye."

When we talk the next day, I'm terse and to the point, not wanting to drag this out or to drag him through the pain. "I gotta be honest about last night. Obviously, I drink. A lot. My problem isn't in the past. Probably never went away ... now that I'm drinking, it's getting bad again."

"Are you using drugs?" He sounds concerned.

"God, no. Just drinking. So far." I threw that in for some added emphasis on how disturbed he should be. "I think I need some time to focus on myself."

The phone line goes quiet except for a faint crackling of static or electricity or whatever moves through phone lines. Sound waves? Yes, crackling sound waves.

"You still there?" I say.

"So ... are you breaking up with me or what?"

"David, I'm sorry but I'm such a mess right now. I can't even begin to tell you." I let out a sigh. "It's better if I'm alone, so I can deal with my drinking." I have no intention of dealing with my drinking. My intention is to drink however and whenever I want without all the secrecy and guilt.

"Why're you doing this? Why won't you let me help? That's what couples do."

Really? Seems to me that being a couple only daylights all of your issues: communication, sexuality, conflict avoidant, conflict seeking, people-pleasing, self-centered, PTSD, co-dependence, you name it. Stay unattached and your issues can lay dormant for years. Get involved with someone and *Bam!* You're painfully aware of all your issues. Your partner is aware of them too. *That* is what couples do.

Besides, I don't want any help. I want to be left alone so I can drink in peace. "David, you can't fix me," I snap.

"I said, *help*, not *fix* you. I don't wanna fix you. You're not broken."

"*Hah!* I am *so* broken. So very broken. You deserve someone who's got their shit together. And that's not me."

The phone line is dead quiet. Not even a sound wave. However, my brain—or brains, seems like there's more than one up there—never shuts up. *He's a good man, and I'm pushing him away. I wasn't even afraid last night, didn't even think about my gun. This is what it feels like to trust a boyfriend. Trust? Boyfriend? What is this shit? You're breaking up with him!*

"Can I call you in a few days?" he asks. "Just to see how you're doin.' Maybe we can talk some more."

Doesn't he know when to cut and run? "You can, but ... nothing will change."

I don't want to quit drinking, and I don't want to keep disguising who I am. If I'm being the real me, David won't want me. I'm certain of that. He won't stay with a woman who is dancing with the devil.

"Are you okay?" I ask. What a stupid question. Of course, he isn't. He's crushed. I'm crushed. He *is* a good man, who I love. We have a shared-life-journey kind of love, a common, academic ambition, but it's not enough. It isn't only his disinterest in backpacking that's missing, though that was a huge hit. I do want that wilderness love. It's me that isn't enough.

"I'll be okay," he says with a catch in his voice. He clears his throat. "I gotta go."

"I'm sor—"

Click. Then a vibrating dial tone, loud and clear.

For days, I keep telling myself, over and over, that David is going to be okay, that I did the right thing and that he deserves someone better. This is the truth, and he will come to see it. Soon, I hope.

My days are full as I distribute my thesis to my committee and schedule a day to defend it. I develop and practice a presentation, and Don runs me through trial questions and answers. My evenings, however, are quiet and lonely. I miss working, reading and studying by David's side. As I'm snuggling with the cats and a six-pack one evening, feeling very gloomy, I find myself thinking, Aww, I want a boyfriend. What the hell? I just had a perfectly decent boyfriend.

Heather and I talk about what happened, but I don't ask her how David is doing. I don't want to know if he's wretched and depressed, or if he already found someone else. As much as I want to reassure myself that he's okay, I don't dare call him. I'm not completely heartless. Besides, David and I didn't bother pretending like we could continue to be friends; that was never going to happen.

Why does everyone say this when they break up, Let's be friends? It's utter bullshit. Being friends after being in love, or having a longish-term sexual relationship, is impossible. The up-close-and-personal knowledge and innermost secrets you share expose that soft underbelly of love. Then when you try to "hangout," all that stuff that you don't dare talk about is hanging out between you, while you're trying to do something mundane like watch *Seinfeld* reruns. No, David and I are never going to watch reruns.

NINETEEN

Fatherly Love

No longer hiding my drinking from David, I'm free to celebrate whenever and however I choose, which is often. I revel in my accomplishments and rightfully so, these are big milestones. I pat myself on the back with a few beers after Don and I have our last practice presentation before my defense. After I successfully defend my thesis in front of five faculty, several grad students and the department chair, I give myself hearty congratulations (several beers, no tequila, though I was tempted). Naturally, I celebrate the day I pick up my Master of Science diploma, which is anticlimactic since there's no ceremony in August. No one is there, not Mom or Floyd or even Don or Warren. The department secretary just hands me the diploma still inside an envelope. My drinking that night is more ceremonious.

Floyd does help me celebrate finally getting that

diploma when he takes me backpacking at Corral Pass. This is the best kind of congratulations, full of laughter, love, berry-picking, stunning views of Mt. Rainier and, later, stargazing. The Milky Way even shows up to applaud me. Sadly, no bears.

When I land a full-time job at the university, that is a Rico's-level achievement. I think I'm onto something here with my achievement drinking; it's like binge drinking but with a purpose. Here's my fail-safe method: 1) I only drink when I reach a milestone. 2) I only consume alcohol, no drugs. 3) For the most part, the Siamese are the only guests joining in the festivities. This way, I won't run into any ex-boyfriends or stumble into any bar-based relationships and don't have to conceal from Heather, Sunita, Isabelle or even Samuel how intensely I'm celebrating. 4) I never let my drinking spill over into my new job, which means I never call in sick and never arrive at work still drunk. On a rare occasion, I show up at work hungover on a Friday morning, but who doesn't?

Jobs have always been a last line of defense. If I can hold down a job, I must be okay. And my work isn't just a job now, this is my career. This new position isn't exactly conflict resolution, but it's in my field, pays more money than I've ever made, will look great on my resume and keeps me at the university where I can start working on publishing my research. I also volunteer at the campus mediation center, helping staff, faculty and students resolve disputes. Also, Warren has started inviting me to work with him as a co-mediator on cases around the state.

These cases are actual environmental disputes with multiple organizations and agencies, sometimes the public. I don't always handle a tense meeting as skillfully as I'd like, but Warren never takes over or criticizes me in front a group. He lets me learn from my mistakes and, afterwards, we talk about how I can improve. Always, he tells me I'm a really good facilitator, a natural at running groups. I'm starting to believe him. Somehow, I have transformed myself from a teenage junkie into someone who can help people deal with serious conflict.

I'm touched (not literally) by these men—Don, Warren, my new boss, Matthew—who are interested in me. Fatherish figures, I guess. They're helping me find success and fulfillment and seeking nothing in return. Bewildering. My man-ometer is so broken.

Warren and I attend a conference in Arizona where we will conduct a two-day conflict resolution workshop for professionals who traveled here from all over the country. At the social mixer before the conference begins, we meet many of the participants who signed up for our workshop: employees of the U.S. Environmental Protection Agency and the National Park Services, and of various state regulatory agencies. These are important people with important jobs in my field, which, I'm becoming aware, is a male-dominated field.

These important people who will attend our workshop tomorrow are mostly men, and every single one of them is older, much older, than me. Teaching eighteen- and nineteen-year-old students is one thing but forty-year-old men? I'm way out of my league. As uncomfortable as I am while mingling, I'm not about to use my old fallback in awkward situations and try to charm any of these men. That would undermine my newfound professionalism, to say the least. I can think of all kinds of damage that could come from a little charm.

As the evening social continues, I become more intimidated, now by the caliber of the other conference presenters. I'm the youngest *and* the least experienced. My stomach is in knots. It doesn't help that the only person I know is Warren. Scanning the room, I see him engaged in a robust conversation with a few people, but can't envision how to subtly elbow my way into that small cluster.

Since Warren can't rescue me, and I've had all the mingling I can stand, I do what any up-and-coming professional would do in this situation: hide.

I hide in the women's restroom for as long as I can without being noticed, which is a long time since there are only like forty women at this conference of two hundred. While I'm stalling in the stall, I wonder if there's a recovery meeting nearby. It's already eight-thirty, and the last meeting of the day usually starts at eight. What finally gets me out of there is remembering the last time I hid in a bathroom, snorting cocaine off the toilet tank. Nothing good ever comes from holing up in a toilet stall.

Back in the event hall, I've morphed from a trained mediator with good skills into an incompetent, unqualified, girl who I despise. Glancing around the room, I notice all the beer bottles and wine glasses. Everyone has one in their hand. All the high-top tables are littered with them. I could get drunk just draining the glasses left on the high-tops—wouldn't that be a sight. The booze is calling, promising to give me all the confidence I need, vowing to restore my credentials and then some. My eyes lock onto the wine and beer table and the young, as in my age, very handsome server. He smiles at me. What could go wrong there?

I've got to get out of here and fast. Just then Warren notices me and waves me over. That gesture is life saver. Exhaling a gush of air and tension, I work my way across the room.

"Isn't this great?" he asks, grinning. Warren is in his element.

"Yeah ... Hey, I'm going up to my room. You have a minute to talk first?"

"Sure. What's up?"

Glancing around the room, I see no empty tables or any space where I can talk without being overhead. "Can we talk in the lobby?"

I don't want to bail on Warren, but I'm hoping he'll let me downplay my teaching role during the training tomorrow because I can't stand in front of all these professional men and act like I have something to offer. I'll just hand out papers, take notes, stuff like that.

"Listen," I say quietly because conference attendees are strolling through the lobby. "I don't know if I can lead my part of the workshop."

Warren, who was leaned back on a sofa, hands crossed

behind his head, pops up straight. "You sick or some-thing?" I suspect he knows what's going on but, being a good mentor, he gives no credence to my insecurities.

"No ... just a little ..." A little wimp, I think, sighing. But I *can't* stand up in front of all these professionals tomor-row. "A little intimidated." I lean in closer, all hushed. "Everyone here's older than me."

"So? Who cares?" He has no tolerance, whatsoever, for even an inkling of discrimination.

"*I* care. These guys—they're *all* men—have worked in the field for years. They're way more experienced—"

"Whoa." He pumps the brakes with his hands. "Hold on. You know more about conflict resolution than all of those people combined. You're one of a handful of experts—"

"I'm *not* an expert."

He glares at me. "Lynn, you're the only grad student I've had who specialized in conflict resolution. All your research, the classes, the trainings, gave you knowledge that took me and others in our field a decade to get."

"Really?" I sit up straighter.

"There still aren't any graduate programs specifically in this field. You're out there in front. On the cutting edge of this stuff."

Heat rises into my face, from embarrassment and doubt and a tiny amount of belief. I start to stammer. "Well ... you know ... you taught me all this ... and you keep letting me work with—"

"Don't do that. Don't downplay yourself and give me,

or anyone else, credit. I wouldn't hire you if you didn't know what you were doing. And those people in there"—he thumbs over his shoulder—"they don't know a thing about resolving conflict. But they have to deal with it in their jobs every day. They're overwhelmed. Their agencies are getting sued. It's a mess. That's why they're taking our workshop."

I still feel inadequate but somewhat stabilized. Warren's belief in me never fails to boost my confidence. Maybe this is what it's like to have a father who has your back, no matter what. Maybe this is what it's like to have fatherly love.

"So, go get a good night's sleep and meet me in the restaurant for breakfast. Seven-thirty sharp." He is a stickler for being on time.

"Yes, sir." I give him a salute and march right past the social hall and the dregs of booze in glasses and the free wine and beer and the handsome server.

Safe! yells the umpire. I'm getting really sick of him.

I am definitely younger than everyone in our workshop, including the four women. While I begin our workshop feeling shaky and nervous, my throat so tight I'm afraid my voice will crack when I talk, by lunchtime, I find my groove. It helps that participants are scribbling notes as I talk—imagine that—and asking lots of questions, for most of which I have answers. During the practice mediations, Warren and I take turns demonstrating how to use various skills in a mock dispute among participants. After the completion of our workshop, we receive nothing but positive feedback and expressions of gratitude from many of the trainees. I float out of that room.

At dinner, Warren orders a beer sampler with a few ounces each of eight different microbrews. He suggests we share it, tasting them all and ordering our favorites. With my self-doubt gone, I decide I can taste a few samples and order a pint of beer. I'm not trying to escape here, just celebrating. At working dinners like this, I always follow Warren's lead on how much to drink. Without knowing it, he's also been mentoring me in the ways of professional drinking. Of course, he's never been to Russia.

When the waiter sits a mouth-watering tray of samples on our table, my butterfly flaps happily. There are two rows, four glasses in each, arranged from lightest, a classic golden colored beer, to darkest, a beer the color of root-beer. I instantly calculate there are thirty-two ounces on the tray, sixteen ounces for each of us. I'm like someone with an eating disorder who can, with a glance, calculate the number of calories on a plate. After my samples, I can only order one pint. The stakes are too high for me to get hammered.

TWENTY

Broken Dreams

After that conference, I buy some business suits but still wish I didn't look so young. I ask Sunita what she thinks about me dying my hair gray at the temples. She laughs and laughs, saying she's going to mark my words on that one. Despite looking younger than my age, to my continued amazement, I seem to command respect in my work. My mediation career is blossoming. I'm living the dream and behaving like a regular person, or how I think one behaves. At least that's how it looks from the outside.

Lurking inside, underneath my business suits and my regular behavior and my non-graying hair, the brain and the butterfly are alive and kicking. Those two sometimes talk me *out* of a twelve-step meeting and often talk me *into* a bar. They usually choose My Office because the scene there is more comfortable than at Rico's. Especially early in the week, say Monday or Tuesday, around five p.m. The ideal setting to unwind.

On my third beer this evening, I'm chatting with the middle-aged, overweight, balding bartender. He tells me how he never finished his degree and never got out of this college town. He has worked there for years.

"You like working here?" I ask, glimpsing an alternate future where I could've been stuck doing the same thing.

He gives me an are-you-kidding, half-cocked smirk. "What d'you think?"

I think life can turn on a dime. If I hadn't gotten that extra funding ... If I'd been offered a job at a bar ... If I'd never finished my master's ... "I think bartending must be a pretty shitty job" I say. "Dealing with drunks, beer fights—"

"That ain't the half of it. Booze makes people crazy. Period. Makes 'em lose all their judgment. Pfft, right out the window." He juts his thumb over his shoulder.

Glancing down at my beer, I regret starting up this conversation, but I'm not about to feel guilty drinking around a bartender. As I take another swig, a gush of fresh air hits my back as someone enters the bar. *Ahh,* that outside air is so refreshing. All bars have the same raunchy smell: cigarette smoke and stale beer and spilled alcohol fermenting everywhere.

"Hey, you," comes a familiar voice behind. Then Alex is standing next to me. He looks good. Too good. He still looks like a Greek god. I'm flooded with a sense of having truly missed him. Then I feel embarrassed as I recall breaking things off with him because we drank too much, while here I sit alone—well, with the bartender—beer in hand. It doesn't matter though because he's with a woman. A cute woman. I've seen her around campus, a couple of times carrying a toddler.

"How *are* you?" I turn toward him, and we give each other a light, quick hug.

"I'm doin' great." He steps back, turns toward the woman. "This is Bethany."

I smile, shake her hand and we say the usuals while Alex orders two beers.

"You still in grad school?" he asks.

"Nope. Finished in August. A little late, as usual. I'm working with Matthew over in the Extension office. And doing some mediation."

He nods. "Right on. Good for you." The bartender sets two beers on the counter. While Alex hands one of the beers to Bethany, he tells me that he worked for the Forest Service over the summer.

Bethany ticks her head. "I'll grab us a booth."

"Be there in a sec," he says. "Just got offered a job in Tennessee. Forestry Department. I'll be moving out there in a couple months."

I glance over at Bethany. "She going with you or—"

"Nah. She's got a little girl and has another year of school. Who knows? She might come out later."

In the awkward pause between us, we both take swigs

from our beers. That part isn't awkward, just like old times. "Glad you found a good job," I say. Take another swig. "The Smoky Mountains out there are beautiful ..."

"Yeah, I think I'll like it. Hey, I'd love to see you before I go. Maybe have a drink"—his eyes flit down to my beer— "or dinner. Lunch. Whatever works."

Let's see: very sultry, Greek god, has girlfriend. This doesn't sound like someone I should have a drink with. Or dinner. "Let's have lunch."

He takes another sip of beer then slowly, while staring right at me, licks the foam off his mustache. "You don't want one last bananas foster?"

Ah! He is shameless. Without a conscience. Indecent. But it works. My nipples jump to attention—traitors. Out of the corner of my eye, I see Bethany watching us. Damned Greek gods and their lusty nature and sumptuous desserts. "I'm on campus every day," I say, all business-like, "in the Extension office. Like I said. Stop by and we can grab lunch. On campus." I all but hand him a business card.

He gives a half-hearted nod. "Alright. I'll stop by before I leave."

I smile and glance in Bethany's direction. "Think she's waiting for you."

With those two in the bar—Alex and Bethany, not my traitorous nipples—I can't drink in peace. To make matters worse, the bartender is playing country music tonight, which I'm not fond of, and now Brooks and Dunn's "Neon Moon" is playing. That song stabs me right in the heart, the goal of all country music, but this one hits a little close to home. I'm not about to sit here, alone, in this rundown bar and watch my broken dreams dance or do anything. No thanks. I'm celebrating tonight, though for what, I forget. I gulp down the rest of my pint and say good-night to the bartender, whose name I also forget.

On my way home, despite the impressive restraint I demonstrated with Alex, I'm aware of how very close I am to the edge. So easily, I could've had a few more drinks and heated things up with Alex, trying to lure him out of that bar. If I was tipsy enough, I would've done all of this right there in front of Bethany. I could've shown that bartender what it really looks like when booze makes someone lose their judgment. (No, he's a bartender; he's seen it all.) I'm teetering on the edge again, this time a very fine edge, a razor's edge, my arms flailing about to maintain balance. On one side of the razor, I can see myself slamming booze and seducing Alex, relinquishing all efforts to control my drinking and my behavior, completely cutting loose. If I cut loose though, I could lose everything. Everything—that's what is on the other side of the razor: an exciting new career, my new friends and a couple of old ones, my family (okay, that's basically only Mom, but she's not no one), a husband and family someday.

Hmm, tough decision. Wobble, wobble.

In the morning, I'm not hungover, but I am unsettled. I head to a twelve-step meeting. This begins a fun merry-go-round ride, in which I bounce in and out of recovery groups as, little by little, I overstep my achievement-drinking boundaries. Either I drink way too much and am hungover for half the next day. Then I go to a twelve-step meeting. Or worse, I go out with friends and, as in my ill-fated Russian fairytale, in the morning can't remember anything. That is always mortifying. If I did something dreadful, I don't want to know; ignorance is bliss or, in this case, face-saving. I only want to know what happened if it wasn't humiliating. Then there's the challenge of how to find out. If I come right out and ask whoever was there, then *they* know that I *don't* know what happened. The whole thing is a lose-lose situation. Then I go to a meeting.

Round and around I go.

Now, having a hangover or a blackout in the privacy of my own apartment—not a problem. At least, not a social problem. Over time, however, it does tend to erode your self-image. The more unpredictable my drinking becomes, the more me-time I suddenly need, also known as hiding. I'm not talking about concealing my drinks or how many I have, or having a couple of starter drinks before I go out with friends for drinks, I'm talking about hiding *myself*. Seclusion. Isolation. Getting plastered alone in my own apartment where the only spectators are the Siamese.

There's something embarrassing about doing things in front of your pets about which you'd *die* if they told someone—binging on and purging food, masturbating, watching *Bewitched* reruns. Luckily, pets can't tell anyone but still, *Bewitched?* It's also demoralizing to sit in your apartment, curtains drawn, getting shit-faced and dancing to all your Van Morrison CDs—played super quietly so no one outside can hear—then refusing to answer the door when one of your caring, nonjudgmental neighbors comes a knocking. Is it so bad to be drinking alone?

I guess so because, after tiptoeing around my apartment yesterday evening, this afternoon, I flat out lie to Sunita. It's our weekend routine: we take our dirty clothes to the laundromat, stuff them in washing machines then walk to the store for a bag of jalapeño chips and a handful of caramel squares. Munching our well-balanced mean, Sunita says, "I came over last night to see if you wanted to have dinner."

I stick another chip in my mouth. *Went to a movie? No, I have no idea what's playing.* Crunch, crunch. "Whoo! These are hot." I pant and wave the spicy heat from my mouth, stalling. "I went to dinner with Isabelle and her boyfriend. Then we went to Rico's."

She plucks another chip from the bag. "I wondered because your car was out back."

Oh, shit! I am *not* going to start hiding my car. What to say? We both are crunch, crunch, crunching these spicy chips that we love, and I love this ritual with Sunita. I love her. I love how she is quick to laughter, love her brilliance and goofiness, her innocence and worldliness. I want so badly to be honest.

"Yeah ... I walked to work yesterday. Isabelle drove us to sushi ..." I despise myself.

She shrugs. "How about dinner tonight?"

I dip my hand into the chip bag and blather on, as if I didn't just tell a bold-faced lie to my dear friend, blather about how dinner tonight would be great and should we meet at her place or mine and what will she make.

My dishonesty with Sunita is more unforgivable than getting smashed, alone, while slinking around in my apartment. This deceit is absurd and unnecessary. I'm not doing anything wrong. Would it kill me to simply put the beer away and answer the door?

I vow not to do either again—slinking or lying—then go to a recovery meeting.

I'm getting woozy on this merry-go-round.

In response to becoming a little sloppy in my fail-safe method of drinking, my definition of a milestone starts to shift. This was bound to happen because I've reached all my big milestones. I'm a professional mediator with a master's degree. I'm coasting in life. I've arrived, so to speak. The bar for what constitutes an "achievement" dropped a little lower. For instance, making it through a difficult workweek is an accomplishment, especially as I'm working longer and longer days (another nifty way to regulate my drinking). Or, say, making it through a challenging Thursday at work. Hell, every time I cobble together a couple of weeks without drinking, I reward myself. With a few drinks.

Being able to stick to my self-imposed limits sometimes, but not always, is also turning into a bit of a merry-go-round. Actually, it's more like a roulette wheel. I'm not sure if I'm the one placing bets or the ball skittering around the roulette. What am I saying? I'm definitely the one placing the bets.

I'm reminded of the psychologist, B.F. Skinner—eight years working at a psychiatric hospital fills your brain with some weird stuff—and his famous lab rats of the 1950s (experimental psychologists and their poor rodents!). His rats pushed a lever, *tap, tap, tap*, sometimes getting a food pellet and sometimes getting nothing. Skinner discovered that when the rats intermittently received a food pellet, they were far more obsessed with pushing the lever than when the rats got a pellet every single time. Getting expected results every time is just ... predictable. You're hungry? *Tap, tap, tap. Yum, yum. Crunch, crunch.* But if you never know when you're going to get a food pellet, if you've tapped many times and got nothing, then you sure as hell better keep trying.

That's me, obsessed with trying to control how I drink because sometimes I can control it and sometimes I can't. Some days, my drinking is normal—well, let's say, without incident. Predictable. And some days, I never know what's going to happen. A crapshoot.

So, I tap away. Tonight, I will not drink myself into a blackout. *Tap, tap, tap.* Tonight, I will not go into a bar. *Tap, tap, tap.* This week, I will not drink until Thursday. *Tap, tap, tap.*

I feel sorry for lab rats everywhere. What choice do

they have but to hit that lever over and over again? And I know exactly how they feel when a pellet doesn't come tumbling down that chute. They feel like they might not survive. They feel a nagging sensation that they are screwed.

#

TWENTY-ONE

Alex doesn't come by my office before he leaves for Tennessee—he comes by my apartment. Zeus, the Greek god of thunder (or lightning or the heavens, at this point, it doesn't matter), is on my doorstep with a six-pack of Full Sail Amber, catnip toys and a won't-take-no-for-an-answer smirk. Trying to fit this scenario into my solitary, achievement-focused drinking, I decide I can make some wiggle room because we *are* celebrating: Alex got a new job and is moving. Plus, there are only six beers, three each.

Zeus sits in my squeaky loveseat, pets the kitties and gives them their catnip. "I couldn't leave without saying good-bye to these beauties." He straightens up and holds my gaze. "Or this one."

Ohhh, do go on! That butterfly is one easy mark.

Snap out of it, I bark at that floozy insect. We're not

falling for that shit, and we're not having sex with this man.

"Thanks for the catnip," I say, revealing none of the internal fluster going on. "So, when's the big day?"

"I leave Monday."

"How's Bethany handling this?"

"We split up. That wasn't gonna go anywhere. She's got a daughter and didn't want her getting attached to me. You know, since I was leaving. She's a good mom." He gives an appreciative nod, which gives me a pang of jealousy. I want to be a good mom someday and have a man who respects that in me. "You still seeing that guy, what's-his-name?"

"David. We broke up a while ago. Before I graduated." I shrug. "It just … didn't work out."

Well, we got all that out of the way quickly, establishing that we're both footloose-and-fancy-free. The two of us couldn't be any more unencumbered. We're friends, we have no partners and he's leaving. This is the one instance in which a guy moving across the country is good news because Alex is bad news. If he moves away, I won't get sucked back into a vortex of heavy drinking. This is all very freeing.

Making himself right at home—gods can get away with that—Alex pops the caps off two bottles, sticks the rest in the fridge and hands me one. He doesn't ask if I want it, and I don't hesitate to take it.

An hour and a half later, we've polished off the six-pack. Got that out of the way pretty quickly too. Five minutes after that, I'm putting our empty bottles in the recycling, disappointed that he didn't bring a twelve-pack, when he comes up behind me.

Heat—simmering, unyielding heat—is radiating from his body. Despite his heat, a shiver runs down my body, from my scalp to my toes and *everywhere* in between. He pushes my hair back, his warm breath under my ear, his mouth on my neck. A hot streak of fire now shoots down the length of my body. We are blazing through the evening, and I'm having trouble regulating my temperature. *Whew!*

Slowly, deliberately he undresses me and, this time, not just with his eyes. No, he undresses me with his hands. *His* clothes come off a bit more quickly.

Between kisses, I say, "I don't—have a—condom." Another of my clever attempts to stay out of the sack with men, which suddenly seems not so clever. Will this save me tonight? Do I need saved? I'm not even tipsy. I'm clear-headed, except for the effect of Alex's heat. That has my head a bit fuzzy. Fuzzy enough that I'm not sure why I didn't want to have sex with him.

Without taking his eyes off of me, Alex picks up his jeans and digs out his wallet. His eyes are roaming all over me, taking me in like he has so many times before, this time while rolling on a condom.

Then he rolls *me* onto my stomach and gently manhandles me into hot, animal sex—doggy style, to be exact, because he wants to see my "perfect ass." Hey, if he insists on referring to my ass as perfect, I'm not stopping him. He gives me a soft bite on my neck, tugs on my nipples, his hands are on my shoulders and down to my waist, pulling me onto him. *Ohhh, Zeus, don't stop. Don't ever stop.* Alex is crooning sweet nothings, okay, dirty, dirty nothings, as we have wild, pagan sex. The Greeks were pagans, weren't they? He grabs hold of my hips and slows his rhythm, moaning my name in a shudder of spasms.

When he leans down and tenderly kisses a path across my shoulders, I explode into an orgasm, shockwaves of heat and release and pulses of ... maybe love.

We collapse onto the bed in a heap—a grinning, unencumbered heap.

"That was definitely worth the wait," he says. "A *year-long* wait." He glares at me, then laughs.

I have just discovered the ideal sex: three-beer sex with a good friend who is moving across the country. Of course, you can only have such ideal sex once or twice, then he's gone. Holiday visits?

Alex runs his fingertips, barely touching my skin, along my spine, from my neck to the small of my back then up again, like a blind man reading the braille of my backbone. What secrets are my vertebrae whispering to him? Something tantalizing, I think, because the hairs on my back are standing on end.

Drowsily, he says, "You know ... I can stay here."

That sounds vaguely encumbered. I don't want him spending the night. In fact, I was thinking about heading out for another six-pack. By myself. "Uh ... I've got some things I have to do for work early tomorrow. I've got this big mediation and I need—"

"Not tonight. I mean I could *stay,* stay." Suddenly, I'm not so relaxed. He turns onto his side and scooches back a bit. He is beaming, even his eyes smile. "You know, not move. To Tennessee."

No, no, no, no. There goes my unfettered sex, my one shot at ideal sex. I'm outraged at him, at me, at us. This is what we get for crossing the line. Friends *can't* be lovers. Not that Alex and I were friends to begin with, more like drinking buddies with some heavy petting thrown in the mix. So, I crossed the friendship line with him a year ago but never this far. And this is what I get. As soon as two happily unencumbered people start rubbing their bodies up against each other, somebody is going to like it better that way, all cozy and intertwined and physical, all moist and heaped up together.

"What are you talking about?" I'm shaking my head. "You can't stay here. You've got a job, a great job. You've gotta move out there." I wave my hand back and forth between our naked bodies. "This was just ..."

His lips clamp into a straight line, and, instantly, my body goes on guard. His eyes go dark, dark, dark, as his pupils dilate.

He's pissed. Get up! Get up! Slowly, so as not to further aggravate the situation, I sit up, swinging my legs off the side of the bed closest to the back door. "At least, I thought this was just sex with a good friend." I slip on my shirt. "Like ... good-bye sex. Terrific good-bye sex."

"Shit. I don't get you." He jumps up and pulls on his pants, shaking his head in dismay. "We have this great sex and you still don't wanna be with me. You're gonna say good-bye like what we did, what we have, is nothing?" He tosses his arms in the air. "You can say good-bye? Just like that?"

Yes, I can. I get it from my father.

I've worked my way closer to the head of my bed, where I keep my gun, and slide into my jeans. I'm so sick and tired of this. Not only the involuntary, heart-pounding fear when I break up with a man (if this can be called a break-up; we weren't even together). I'm tired of men wanting more from me than I have to give. Tired of hiding who I am and feeling guilty about it. I'm tired of hating both, who I'm pretending to be and who I really am.

Why can't a relationship with a man be simple, like work is? I learned how to be a pretty damned good mediator in a matter of a few years, but I've been involved with or dating men—whatever you want to call it—for over a decade, and I'm still no good. Even when Heather, the best matchmaker I could hope for, did the picking, I screwed everything up. Most of the adult world is paired up, in some form or another, for big chunks of their lives. I want a husband, a family, a cool house, a mountain view, a yard with a dark night sky, a little passion. What am I doing wrong, and where are the god-damned instructions?

"I'm sorry this happened." I sweep my hand over the bed. "I didn't think it would change any—"

"It changes *everything.* I wanna be with you. I love you."

Great! Cupid is here. Well, I'm yanking his arrow right out of Zeus' heart because I can handle Alex's physicality and his sexiness and his decadent desserts but not his love. I may not know what love is but have to believe I'll know it when I feel it, and I don't feel it for Alex. What I experienced with him was pagan love: wild and animal and ... fleeting. He's a Mediterranean lover not a boyfriend.

"Nothing's changed for me," I say softly. "I don't want a relationship based on partying and sex." Did I just say that? My previous therapist, Miriam, would be so proud.

My brain howls at me. *What are you talking about?* All *of your relationships have been based on sex.*

Go fuck yourself, I tell my brain.

Alex is indignant. "We've known each for, what, two years, and this is the first time we've had sex. How is that a relationship based on sex?"

Okaaay. I stand corrected. "When we were hanging out last year, we were mauling each other. Getting drunk and mauling each other. We did everything *but* have sex. This right here, what's happening, is why I never wanted to have sex because I don't wanna hurt you. But I don't want to be a couple. I'm sorry. I don't feel that way about you." I don't insult him further with the let's-just-be-friends B.S.

He stares at me for a few moments. I hold his gaze as long as I can without seeming like I'm having a stare-down. I can see him swallow hard, his Adam's apple sliding down his throat. "I'm gonna give the kitties a snuggle before I go, alright?"

That levels me. This is one of Alex's qualities that I find rare in a man: he cherishes my cats.

He finishes dressing then nestles between the girls, a hand on each one, and closes his eyes as if channeling to them love and health and nine long lives. Watching his tenderness with my cats calms my PTSD-hypervigilant lizard brain—that reptile is really starting to embarrass me. I can't believe that I thought, for one second, that Alex could hurt me.

When he stands, his face looks crumpled. He hugs me tightly. "I'm gonna miss you so much," he whispers. "Take care, okay? Just take care of yourself."

I nod, as well as I can in his embrace. He doesn't look at me, just unwraps his arms from around me and leaves.

Now that *that* is all over, I don't want any more beer; I just want to go to bed. Not because I'm tired, but because I need retreat, the cave that only a bed can provide. Curled under the blankets, I begin to cry. I'm not even sure why I'm crying. Maybe because I *will* miss Alex because he gives great, big bear hugs and loves my cats and is a decent guy. Or maybe because, where men are concerned, I'm broken. Hopelessly broken.

I wake without a hangover and with complete recall of the night before. Nothing like a crystalline, stone-cold, sober morning staring you in the face, nothing fuzzy about the night before, only the stark clarity of having sex with a friend who loves you, then dumping him. Again. I'm a selfish, awful person. I knew I didn't want Alex and resisted this, resisted him, for over a year. So why did I give in? And I wasn't drunk so can't use that excuse. This makes no sense. Is this what people mean when they say, It just, sort of, happened? No, I know better. Sex doesn't just happen. Except when I'm loaded; when I'm loaded anything can "just happen." But I wasn't loaded last night. I had three beers.

After my pathetic night of barely drinking and still being a fuck-up, I can barely stand to be in the same room with myself. I don't want to drink, which is baffling because I know how to get rid of self-loathing. I know how to take away any feeling: fear, shame, embarrassment, boredom, sore throat. That is the great promise of alcohol and drugs: I can change the way I feel in thirty minutes flat. Hell, with the right buzz, I can change the way I look, and I'm not talking about putting on make-up. I can prove to myself that I'm desirable by becoming sultry and seductive, capturing the attention of some lonely man at a bar (and we all know how difficult that is). A good buzz and *Snap!* I'm transformed. Self-doubting to confident. Fearful to brazen. Unworthy to irresistible.

This morning, the facts are glaringly clear: alcohol is a teasing seductress, one that never delivers. Using mood-altering substances is all smoke and mirrors, a pipedream wherein I feel on top of the world and amazing, for a few hours, then I'm circling the drain, getting pulled into another whirlpool.

That evening, still not drinking, I go to a recovery

meeting. On the way to the meeting, I rehearse what I want to say, I practice being honest enough to get some ... not help, I'm not asking for help ... some relief. I want relief. I need relief. If I was Catholic, I'd go to confession. Anything to get a break from this self-loathing, to stop me from reliving last night (and not the good part). All day, I relive my crushing of Alex's spirit. Over and over, I see his crumpled face when he said good-bye to the kitties. And to me.

At the meeting, I can hardly wait for my turn to talk, bouncing my foot under the table, gnawing and picking on my cuticles, willing others to shut the hell up. I'm the picture of serenity.

As soon as I open my mouth, words start pouring out, words I didn't plan on saying, words I didn't rehearse. "I relapsed, if you can call it that. I had five and half years clean and sober then, two years ago, started drinking again. I've been trying to control it ever since. The problem is, I don't want to control it. I don't want just a few, I want to get shit-faced. But then I end up doing something I regret. Or have a blackout." I shake my head and stare out in front of me at nothing. "God ... those suck. Then I'm back in here again with you fuckin' people."

"*Geez*, thanks a lot," mutters Rebecca, one of the regulars.

My fury flares. I don't need her judgment and criticism. But as quickly as it flashes, my fury dies down. After all, what did these fuckin' people ever do to me? Listen?

Give me their phone numbers? Offer me help and hope? How dare they!

"Sorry," I continue, "I just hate this vicious circle. I hate addiction. All I wanna do is get drunk and not get in trouble."

Rebecca then shares about a horrific night she spent in a fraternity that finally forced her to accept that she can't put any kind of drugs or alcohol in her body and have any control over what happens. She tells the group, even when life is great, she knows that she is only one drink or drug away from a frat house.

Frat houses are notorious places where problem drinkers reach their bottoms, metaphorical ones (though there's lots of reaching at frat houses for real bottoms, women's). What sticks with me about Rebecca's story isn't the horror of a fraternity—my night at a frat was just the beginning, my drinking got ever so much worse—but the notion of being *one* drink away from my worst night. One drink?

Other people in meetings have said things like, It's the first drink that gets them drunk, to which I always thought, What a bunch of lightweights. For me, it's the fourth or fifth drink. This first drink, one drink crap keeps popping into my mind long after I leave the meeting because I don't understand it. One drink never got me into trouble. One cigarette, sure, because the damned things come in packs of twenty. What am I supposed to do with the other nineteen cigs, throw them out? You know what a pack of cigarettes costs? I'll finish this pack, then I'll quit smoking again. For the umpteenth time. But one drink, no matter how fast I chugged it, even one shot of tequila, right down the hatch, never got me drunk. One drink might make me warm and glowy, but even social drinkers feel that way after one drink. (These social drinkers with their, Whoa! No more for me; I'm starting to feel it. To which I say, Don't stop now. You're getting to the good part!)

Where alcohol consumption is concerned, I don't understand anyone: not the recovering problem drinkers or the normal, social drinkers, and I sure as hell don't understand myself. For an educated, intelligent woman, I sure am dense.

TWENTY-TWO

End of the Line

Trying to figure myself out, I start going to the same meeting just about every week. There are a handful of regulars here who have all this connection and comradery. I'm out there doing hard time —getting hammered, alone—while they're in here laughing and joking and hugging and being real with each other. These fuckin' people.

The regulars are onto me and know that I'm still drinking. Recovering addicts recognize someone who is still suffering. They see my defeated spirit, my glassy, bloodshot eyes, my pale skin—signs of a brutal hangover. I've been in their position before, watching someone scuttle into a meeting, exhausted from being slapped around by drugs and alcohol but still not ready to stop.

Despite the regulars seeing right through me, I don't introduce myself as a newcomer or talk about my latest misery. I don't share that I'm actively drinking. After my last burst of honesty at a meeting, I rarely speak up. But I do listen. A few things I hear *are* starting to sink in. One idea in particular makes a lot of sense: just don't pick up a drink or drug *today*.

This mundane little suggestion works on any compulsion. Give yourself permission to drink all the booze, eat all the cookies, buy all the clothes, gamble your house away—tomorrow. But don't go near any of it today. When you get *really* nuts about the booze or the food or the stuff, when your brain or body or wallet is screaming for a fix, give yourself permission to have it in one hour, just not right now. Then, in one hour, postpone your fix for another hour.

In my early twenties, I got off the cocaine in this very way, one hour at a time. When I quit smoking, it was five minutes at a time.

The reason this trick works, even though it's counterintuitive, is that I can refrain from doing pretty much anything for a few minutes or an hour. Then for a few more minutes. But if I tell myself I'm *never* having another drink or drug, that seems impossible so why bother trying.

The other reason this trick works is because it's the exact opposite of my brain's great idea, which is something like, Go ahead, have a drink (or cigarette or pint of ice cream). You can always quit tomorrow. Then tomorrow, my brain says, Go ahead, have a drink …

So, using my keen intellectual powers—I mean, this simple little trick— I cobble together several weeks without drinking. Then I blow it, as usual. (Listened to my brain that day.) This doesn't stop me from touting it, all wise and cool, in meetings, saying things like: I'm not using any substances today, and Just for today ... However, the true meaning of *my* words when I say that I'm not drinking today is often: I drank last night. But let's not mince words here.

Another thing that is sinking in each time I sit in a meeting is that I am furious. Not because I drank too much the night or week before—I gave up the delusion that I can have a just few and unwind. Screw normal drinking. I want to leave myself behind and soar. I'm furious because every time I put alcohol in my body, I have no idea what will happen. An evening, sometimes an afternoon, of drinking can be perfectly uneventful or painfully remorseful or a complete blank space. Truly, anything can happen.

Only I don't give a shit anymore what I drink or how much or how often. Like a person on a diet who finally succumbs to the chocolate cake and, with the diet now blown for the day, says, Screw it. Screw the calories and the celery and the one-inch cubes of cheese. Bring me a slab of chocolate cake! Bring me another drink because I'm trying to soar here—without any humiliating or dangerous aftermath. Is that really too much to ask?

When I was nineteen or twenty, before I ever tried to go one day or one hour without drinking, I was driving home from a bar when a policeman pulled me over. He asked me to step out of the car for a sobriety test. Stand on one foot, tip my head back and touch my nose. After the third try, I giggled and said I couldn't even do that sober. The officer shook his head and told me to drive straight home. Wow, what a hard-ass. It's shocking that I was only pulled over once, given that I drove anytime I went out drinking. In my typical intoxicated condition, I could never figure out how else to get home. Getting in a car with some guy from the bar never ended well.

Since that time, drunk-driving laws got strict, and cops are actually enforcing them—thank goodness. Also, this small town where I now live is not Columbus Ohio. It would be impossible to careen around the streets here, plastered, and not be noticed by a cop—thank goodness. Also, drunk drivers kill people, and that's a risk I'm not willing to take—thank goodness. I absolutely will not drive while under the influence.

Besides, I can walk to any bar in this town in less than twenty minutes.

Tonight, I'm walking home from Rico's when a bus passes me then pulls to the curb up ahead. As I near the front of the bus, the door hisses open. In the driver's seat is a scrappy looking guy with mischievous eyes. He has a patchy beard, unkempt hair jutting out in all directions from underneath a well-worn, green ski cap. He is cute in a wiry leprechaun sort of way. I smile. Perhaps he's my lucky charm.

He hollers down to me. "You gettin' on or what?" It's snowing and the wind is cutting through my coat and hat. I never rode the bus here, could be an adventure. Plus, warm air is billowing out of the bus.

I climb up the steps, the door clamps shut behind me and the bus bumps on down the road. I'm lurching down the aisle, holding the rail above my head, when I realize the bus is empty. I stop right there in the middle of the bus. Red flag warning: alone, at night, with a man, in a place I can't easily escape. Then the bus slows near the next stop, no one is there, so the bus picks up speed again. Oh, I can get off at any stop, I think. No problem. This is one of the curses of mind-numbing alcohol, it takes away *all* your worries, even the ones you maybe should pay attention to.

I sway—from the booze and the lumbering bus—back to the last row and sit in the middle, my legs stretched into the aisle. Having no idea where the bus or I am headed, I think, What the hell. I could use an adventure, a little tour of the town.

Two women get on at the next stop, then get off three stops later. One very studious looking man rides for a while. Periodically, Lucky Charm glances at me in the monstrous rearview mirror mounted above little green ski cap. I try to give him my sexy look but am having trouble keeping my eyes open.

What startles me awake is the silence and stillness of

the bus, no more rumbling engine or blowing heater. I blink and look around, trying to get my bearings. Lucky Charm shifts around to face me. "Where were you headed?"

"Was goin' home." In the darkness, I can make out another bus and a chain link fence. "Must've fallen asleep. Where are we?"

"Bus depot. I'm done with my route. All the buses are done."

I have no idea where the bus depot is or why the hell he let me stay on the bus. What did he think he was going to do with me once his run was over? Maybe he asked if I wanted off at his last few stops, and maybe I kept saying, No, not this one. Nope. Nope. Could be I sat in the back flirting shamelessly with him. Or maybe I passed out.

"What time is it?" I ask.

"Nine o'clock. I'm goin' to Shermer's for a bite to eat, few drinks"—My brain snaps to attention. *Drinks?*—"if you wanna come." He sounds indifferent, like he couldn't care less what I do.

I scan the dark parking lot again. A street light is shining onto the sidewalk outside the fence. The chain link transports me back to a dark night on the streets of downtown Columbus when I was a thirteen-year-old runaway looking for my next drink or drug. My best option that night was a carnie with rotting teeth.

"C'mon," Lucky Charm smiles. "I'll buy you a drink."

At least he has nice teeth, I think. But booze gets me tangled up with men. This time won't be any different.

My brain jabs me. *You heard the man. Drinks!*

Shermer's reeks of chicken strips and French fries cooked in too-old grease. A handful of people are there, most of them in their thirties. An old man sitting at the bar waves Lucky Charm over.

"Good to see you," says the old guy.

"What're you doin' here?" Lucky Charm leans over and hugs the old man. "Thought your doctor told you to lay off the booze?"

The old man waves the question away. "Screw 'em doctors. What d'they know." I bet the doctors know you're in liver failure, I think. That's my diagnosis from the looks of this shriveled-up man—skinny body, bloated belly, yellowish hue to his skin and eyes. Then he points at me. "Hey pretty lady. Can I buy ya wine cooler?" He giggles and pats his stomach. "Tha's all my gut can take anymore."

"No, I'm fine," I say because I've never been a fan of wine coolers: sweet, pink, fizzy and no kick whatsoever. Bunch of calories and no high. No thanks.

"I insist." He heads to the bartender at the far end of the bar.

"Hey, Howard," Lucky Charm calls after him. "We're gonna grab a table."

As we slide into a booth, he glances back over at Howard. "He's a great guy. Not supposed to be drinking, but he won't stop. Doesn't matter what anybody says. I don't think he *can* stop." Hearing this gives me a dry lump in my throat.

Howard staggers toward our table, his hands wrapped around a jumble of wine coolers—four of them. With any luck, he'll drop mine. He scooches into our booth with all four bottles, regrettably, and slides one to me and one to Lucky Charm. Snickering, he says, "Tha' bartender's too slow. Got my next one while I was up there." Then he cups his hands around the other two wine coolers and pulls them close, smiling at them like they're his long-lost children finally come home. Howard is having a love affair with pink fizzies.

Ohh, I know this love. For many years, this was the only love I knew. This is the love of dreams that go nowhere and promises that never come true. This is the love that leaves no room for any other love. This could become the love of my wasted life.

Howard is at the part of inebriation where he is floating, full of bliss and doesn't care about any consequences. He can't even begin to conjure the remorse that will surely come in the morning, if not later tonight. As effervescent as his wine coolers, Howard babbles on and on, so that it's hard for Lucky Charm or I to get a word in. I don't mind because I don't want to get to know the bus driver, though I'm sure he's a charming guy.

I chug my wine cooler, which does zilch to restore my buzz. I am crashing. I'm on an end-of-the-bus-line date, which must truly be *the* end of the line as far as dating goes, if you could even call this a date. A bloated, old man next to me is killing himself with alcohol. None of this is doing anything for the lump in my throat. I'm choking on my reality.

Lucky Charm stands and stretches. "I'm gonna get some food and a real drink. Want anything?"

I jump out of the booth. "I'll go with you and see what they have on tap."

"What d'you want?" he says to Howard.

My eyes grow wide with astonishment. This man shouldn't be drinking. The guy's liver is shutting down before our eyes. Why is he offering to buy this poor man more booze?

Howard leans his face closer to his wine cooler then pulls back from it, trying to focus on it to determine if he's ready for another one. "I'm good." He gives a little salute then an uninhibited belch that smells pink and fizzy.

By the time Lucky Charm and I finish chicken strips, fries and a couple of beers, Shermer's is getting crowded and raucous. A woman scrambles up onto a table and starts dancing. As she pumps her arms in the air to Bruce Springsteen's "Dancing in the Dark," her shirt creeps up, exposing belly rolls muffining over top of her jeans. There's definitely somethin' happenin' somewhere for her. She isn't fifty and bombed in a small town. In her mind, she is young and alive and sexy.

The bartender yells at her. "Get the hell off that table or get outta here!"

"Awww, fuck off," she slurs.

The bartender rolls his eyes. "Just get down from there before you break your fuckin' neck, will ya?"

What a lovely place!

Springsteen's voice trails off and so does her zeal for dancing in the dark. She juts her chin out triumphantly at the bartender. "Fav'rite song's over anyways." Surveying the table under her, she teeters down onto her hands and knees, then onto her belly and slides off the table.

I know the magic of being transformed by alcohol, but it's not happening for me tonight. Maybe because I lost my earlier high from Rico's then picked back up here—too much time between buzzes. Maybe my burning indigestion from greasy chicken strips destroyed my high. Regardless of the reason, I'm not reaching the oblivion that makes me and my world the best it's ever been. My world is staring me right in the face. I survey my own table with the listless, disheveled bus driver and his booze-happy friend who is drinking himself to death.

I can't do this anymore. My life is finally getting started, and this drinking is going to grind it to a halt. Tomorrow, actually today, since it's after midnight, I'm going to a recovery meeting. The first one I can find. If necessary, the one with the preppy college kids.

Leaning into Lucky Charm—I still don't know his name, and it'd be rude to ask now—I say, "I need to get home. And the buses are done for the night." That gets a little snort out of him. "You good to drive or ... how many drinks've you had?"

He holds up three fingers. "If you count a wine cooler as a drink. I'm good." He doesn't even polish off his second beer before giving Howard a couple of pats on the shoulder. Howard's body sways with each pat.

"What about him?" I ask.

"He always walks home."

That's exactly what I should do, I think.

TWENTY-THREE
Six Hours Later

The next thing I know, I wake up in Lucky Charm's bed. Oh, fuck no!

Sheee's out! yells the umpire, his fist clenched the air.

My brain starts right in with the tsking and the head-shaking, rattling off unsolicited, condescending advice. *Now look what you've done. You're gonna have to get an HIV test—*

Shut up, I scream at my brain. You're the one that got me into this mess to begin with! No good, useless brain.

Okay, okay. Think, think. I need to think. I just had my period. Can't get pregnant. But STDs—damn it. I should ask him if we had sex. What other choice do I have? *Ohh, this is going to be so humiliating. What am I going to say? Ahem. Excuse me. Uh, strange man whose name I don't know. One teensy question, if you please. Did you screw me last night and, if so, did you by chance use a condom?*

Carefully, slowly, I sit up. My hangover is shattering: head throbbing, body sweating, throat scorched, mouth salivating in response to the bile roiling in my stomach. His place reeks of years of stale cigarette smoke, further nauseating me.

My not-so-lucky charm opens his eyes and looks over at me without moving anything, not even his head. Only his eyes roll over in my direction, which kind of freaks me out, like he's paralyzed. Or maybe he's also devastated to wake up in bed next to a stranger. Nah, I don't think that bothers men.

"I gotta get home," I say. "Did I ... is my car here?" Wherever here is.

He presses his fingers against the bridge of his nose. Good, he isn't paralyzed. "I drove. Don't know where your car is. At your place, I guess. You got on my bus last night."

Oh, right. The bus driver. I went home with the bus driver. *Ughh! How did I let this happen? I'm a grown woman. With a career. I was part of a professional delegation to post-Soviet-Union Russia. I don't do this anymore.*

As I'm dressing, I have a physical urge to flog myself with my jeans, my purse, better yet my boots, anything to knock some sense into my stupid, stupid brain. What is wrong with me? I'm a sleaze. I don't even know where I am. How far can I be from my place in a small town like this ... unless he lives out in the country? Then he'll have to take me home—hopefully not by bus. Holy shit, we could be out in the boonies. He could be planning on holding me hostage.

Leaning against his window sill while I pull on my boots, I peek out the window. Houses all around. Good, I'm not a hostage.

He sits up in bed, his back against the wall, and lights a cigarette. "Want some breakfast?" His tone is inviting, a little sexy sounding, oblivious to the panic attack I'm having.

I shake my head, thinking, Don't even try it. You're not getting laid again this morning, if you got laid last night. All I can do is hope that he didn't, hope that I was so hammered, he just let me sleep. *Righhht.* I've got to find out if we had sex. There's only one way.

"Hey, things are a little fuzzy from last night," I start. He grins. Not a good sign. "Did we … um … sorry, I drank a lot yesterday. Before Shermer's. So, I … don't remember everything. Did we have sex?" Probably not what a man wants to hear in the morning, that he was not memorable. But I have more pressing matters here than his ego.

He looks as uncomfortable as I feel. "We did."

"Did you wear a condom?" *Please, please, please, and I will never do this again.*

"I did." He sounds a bit insulted.

Thank you, thank you, thank you. "That's a relief," I say, releasing a sigh. He stares at me, looking quite insulted. "You know, birth control wise," I add helpfully.

"I don't have HIV," he snaps.

This is one of the most horrific conversations I think I've ever had.

"No STDs here either." I chuckle, embarrassed and

trying to lighten the mood because his prickly tone is unsettling.

"Hey, I'm gonna pass on breakfast," I say, though I doubt his offer still stands. "I just gotta go. My cats, poor things, must be starving." No food since the kibble I left in their bowls yesterday morning. I'm not even a decent cat lady.

"Cats? Let's go then." He throws back the covers and gets out of bed.

Is he mocking me? Pissed and mocking me?

Pulling on his pants, he says, "C'mon. I'll take you home. Where d'you live?" Not much in life is as degrading as a man asking where you live while pulling on his pants.

"No, that's okay."

"But the cats ..." He's looking around the floor, for his shirt, I assume.

I still can't tell if he is serious or ridiculing me. "I wanna walk, clear my head."

"Alright." He shrugs then reaches toward the night-stand drawer. "But can I—"

Nightstand. Maybe a gun. Move! Move! I rush out of the room and head down the hall. There. Front door.

"Hey," he calls after me. "Lemme get your phone number before you go." He catches up with me in the front room, still shirtless, holding a scrap of paper and a pen.

My hand is already on the door knob. My heart is racing. *Just go. Get out!* Some other part of my brain says, You had sex with the guy. You can't refuse to give him your number. That's just plain slutty.

Who are all these people?

When I pull the door open, freezing air is sucked inside, rushing into my open coat and under my sweaty armpits, sending a chill down my back. A cold blast of freedom. I'm halfway out the door when the part of my brain that, evidently, cares more about my reputation than my life pauses to rattle off my phone number.

The sharpness gone from his voice now, he sounds more optimistic. "I'll call you. Maybe we can go out for dinner."

Hurrying away from his house, I say, "I'm swamped with work right now but ... sure. Give me a call."

Glancing over my shoulder to make sure he isn't watching me, I pick up my pace, walking as fast as I can, like a power walker only without the arm pumping. My head can't take the pounding and the sidewalk is icy, but I want to get as far away from his house as quickly as possible. Hungry cats are waiting. Also, I don't want to be seen by anyone I know. Who power walks at six-thirty on Sunday morning?

And I thought it was dangerous to drink and drive. I will *never* again drink and bus-ride.

TWENTY-FOUR

Obsessions

S afely at home, I'm no longer panicked about my night with a stranger. I'm hopeless. This can't be happening again. It was unacceptable when I was younger, but I'm almost thirty. And to think, I'm trying to find a husband. Mercy! I must be losing my mind. I need help, serious help. Therapeutic help.

I could call Miriam, my shrink from Ohio. In my early twenties, she pulled me back from the brink of crazy. When I moved away, she told me I could always call. She probably knew I wouldn't make it out here, knew I wasn't ready. If I want her help, I'd have to tell her how far I've backslid. All our hard work, down the drain. The thought of rehashing with her all of my recent debauchery makes me more despondent.

Disgusted and exhausted, I drop into bed and sleep until noon.

When I awake, my hangover has faded. Things always

look worse from the dark pit of a hangover. Now, things don't seem as bleak. It could've been so much worse—I could've done something illegal or hurt someone. The cats seem to have forgiven me. I decide to see how I feel during the week. If I'm still a basket case in a few days, I'll call Miriam.

For the next two days, I don't drink a drop of alcohol and, mercifully, don't hear from the bus driver. To occupy my days and my mind, I'm collaborating with several environmental experts to write a technical document, which I work on ten to twelve hours a day. When my hateful brain starts in with the If-they-only-knew-what-you-did-over-the-weekend crap, I dig into my project more deeply: call another expert, send them a draft section of the document to review.

During my lunch break, I volunteer on a case at the university mediation center. It's a very emotional, long-standing conflict between a staff person and her boss. At one point, the staff person runs out of the room in tears but, in the end, agrees to another mediation.

My new workaholism is quite effective at helping me ignore my problems—alcohol, men, buses. Overworking provides all kinds of opportunity—a socially acceptable one, for a change—to bury my head in the sand and escape my self-hatred. I highly recommend workaholism; four out of five stars. However, cats will give it zero stars. Families too, I'm sure.

The irony that I can help people in sensitive and tense professional settings, when a few days ago I went home with the bus driver, is not lost on me. The contrast makes me feel more like a fraud than ever and more than slightly nuts. Concealing parts of myself so completely reminds me of a multiple personality patient in the hospital where I used to work. That makes me think, again, of Miriam. Not sure it's a good sign when insanity reminds you of your shrink. But I still don't want to tell her how I've crashed and burned. Telling her the truth will make it real, and I don't want this to be real.

Later in the week, while I'm still waffling about calling Miriam, the bus driver calls. "Hey, it's me, James. Your friendly neighborhood bus driver."

James! His name is James. I can't bring myself to brush him off because that would make what we did a one-night stand, and I don't do that anymore. Absurdly, I agree to go out with him for Chinese food. Anything but Shermer's because I'm not drinking one drop. This thing, whatever it is, with James is *not* turning into a two-night stand. My intention is to come up with a good explanation as to why I can't see him or sleep with him anymore.

When James gets out of his car, he doesn't see me waiting out front—I'm not introducing him to the Siamese. He checks his reflection in the car window, runs his hand through his hair, even clears his throat as he walks up to my apartment. There's something chivalrous, even sensitive, about those gestures. Guess I don't need the gun that's in my purse, but I always take it when I go out with someone new. Yes, even if I just slept with him. Be prepared or be scared. Such a fun perspective for life.

James is self-possessed, irreverent and a little ... not shy more cautious and halting. He acts like he's afraid to spook the herd; as if he might say or do the wrong thing, and I'll bolt. Either he is highly intuitive or he had someone bolt on him before.

In defense of my unforgivable behavior last weekend with the bus driver, it turns out James is no ordinary bus driver. He got sick of the city not offering bus service between high priority locations for students, so he got an old bus, painted "Free" on the side and started driving students around until the city got its act together and started a new route. They hired James as one of the drivers. He is a get-shit-done kind of person. I like that in a bus driver.

As far as boyfriends go, however, James isn't my type. For one, he smokes. I'm an ex-smoker and plan to stay that way. A few other no-go qualities: he has no interest in education, the only outdoor activity he likes is fishing and he has no significant plans for the future. It sounds like the only place he'll go anytime soon is to the next bus stop.

Despite my intentions to say good-bye to James and to avoid drinking, after dinner, we end up back at Shermer's. *Who is in charge here?* Wine Cooler Howard is there and wags his finger at me. "I 'member you. You seein' my frien' here?" He elbows James. "He—is—t'rrific." He works hard to get those words out, but his next words roll right off his tongue. Y'all wanna cooler?"

"No, thanks. I'm good," I say, though drinking

watered-down, fizzy wine is about the same as not drinking at all, which is exactly what I plan to do.

James also declines a wine cooler and asks if I want a beer. Behind the bar, there are rows and rows of bottles. There's the Jose Cuervo tequila. What I want is a shot of tequila. This is one of the few reasons to come to a place like Shermer's: they serve cheap, hard liquor and lots of it. This may be the only reason. Unless you're looking for greasy-food heartburn or want to visit with a jaundiced, bloated man who, by nine p.m., can barely walk or talk. Oh, there may be table-top dancers later.

For all the longing and fear that tequila arouses in me, it might as well be a half-kilo of cocaine stuffed between the Jim Beam and Jack Daniels. It will provide instant joy, a jolt of happiness right to my brain, but might leave me with a dark, empty void in place of my memory. A black hole that could be filled with me table-top dancing. Or much, much worse.

"Can you get me a hot tea?" I say.

James' bushy eyebrows rise up. "Like Lipton or somethin'?"

"Yeah. Little white bags, cup of hot water." I make the dunking motion. As if no one ever ordered tea in this classy joint.

Howard slurs on about something that I barely hear because my mind is locked onto the Jose Cuervo that I didn't order. I peek over his shoulder at the bottles glinting. My pulse increases.

James returns with a bottle of beer and a mug of hot

tea. He invites Howard to join us at a table. What a romancer, this James, looping Howard into our date. Is it a date when you go out for dinner the week after you had sex with a stranger?

As the three of us talk, I'm gripped by the salt shaker on the table, an essential ingredient of drinking tequila, which I'm not. I envision licking my hand on the fold between my thumb and index finger, sprinkling salt on the moistness, then licking it off right before I slam back a shot of tequila. I imagine the tart lime squirting into my mouth as I bite into it, chasing the tequila shot. A shiver runs down my back at the mere thought of the sourness. My mouth waters. All the noise around me becomes a murmur, even the bar smells are muted, by my fantasy of tequila. *This is nuts. I should go home.*

James is waving his hand in front of me, saying, Yoo-hoo, to get my attention. I zoom back into the bar with the blaring music, people shouting over it and Howard's slob-bery stupor. James has finished his beer and asking if I want anything else. I take a sip of my flavorless, now luke-warm tea. This is no Russian Caravan tea.

Speaking of Russia, I say to myself, you can handle *one* shot of tequila. Hell, you drank several shots of vodka in Russia, on numerous evenings, and only had one blackout. You're now a professional mediator. With a master's degree. You can handle this. It's only one ounce. Plus citrus fruit.

I tell James I'd like a shot of tequila with lime. It comes

out decisively, quickly before I change my mind. James heads to the bar with my harmless order.

Howard shudders and lets out a painful sounding grunt. "*Mmhh.* Gave tha' stuff up long time ago."

I stare at him for a few beats. "Too hard on your gut?"

He gets a far-off look on his face, maybe sad or remorseful. Frowning, he says, "*Nawww.* Tha' wasn't it ..."

Oh, please stop right there. "Well, you got your coolers now," I say, usefully. That seems to snap him out of his reverie, and he looks down at his cooler and grins.

We spend another hour there, and I pay zero attention to anything because I'm mesmerized by the tequila sitting in front of me. One ounce. And a citrus wedge. Good, I won't get scurvy. The way my brain carries on about it, you'd think it was poison. Or water. *I can't drink this. You can't waste it, he paid for it. I'll give it to him then. Oh, stop being a wussy and drink it. I don't wanna end up like Wine Cooler over there. Aw, you can always quit tomorrow. Tomorrow? If I drink it, I could wake up in Nebraska.*

Fuck, it's getting crowded up there.

This is the moment—more like the hour—when I realize that I am truly obsessed with alcohol. I've long known that I can do embarrassing or humiliating things when I'm smashed, but that can happen to anyone who overindulges. Have one too many drinks, mix in a little bad judgment about how tipsy you are and voilà—a DUI. Sitting there staring at that shot though, I understand, not just intellectually but in my bones, that I don't control alcohol. Alcohol controls me.

For the past two years, I've been dancing with alcohol, and I'm clearly not in the lead. I'm being dragged around the floor like one of those women during a 1920s-dance marathon who, bedraggled and exhausted, is hanging limply from her partner's arms. I'm in a dancing-with-the-devil marathon.

In the morning, I'm stunned that I can't remember what happened to that damned shot of tequila and not because I blacked out. I'm in my own bed and know how I got here—James dropped me off after I declined his very generous offer that I spend the night at his place. I recall the shot glass in front of me, the golden-colored tequila glowing. I see the salt shaker at the ready (no salt-encrusted shot glasses at Shermer's). I remember the bar noises: the murmur of James and Howard, the clang of glasses, the bellows and hoots of drunks, the pumping beat of music. But did I drink the tequila? Given my preoccupation with that shot, I would certainly remember if I drank it, so I must not have. On the other hand, I have never, ever, left a perfectly good buzz sitting on a table.

Having a blank spot about part of an evening because I was fixated on a shot of tequila is more than a little unsettling. A blackout I can understand, but an obsess-out? I really am going crazy.

TWENTY-FIVE

Someone to Worry About You

B efore I lose my courage, I get up Monday at five a.m., eight a.m. Ohio time, to call Miriam. I'm going to be completely honest before I get sucking into a whirlpool of booze and obsessive thinking and men.

Her assistant answers. "Doctor Adler's in the office, but she's with a client. I'll give her the message that you called."

All the courage seeps right out of me, and I could sob. "Oh ... um ..."

"It'll probably be an hour or two before she calls back. You okay to wait?"

"*Mm-huh.* I'll be okay." That's all the courage I can choke out.

When the phone rings an hour later and I hear Miriam's voice, the tears flood out of me. Snot too. The very picture of courage.

She lets me cry it out, then says, "Tell me what's going on."

Stretching the phone cord into the kitchen, I snag a paper towel to wipe off the snot. "I'm drinking again." *Really? That was my big moment of truth?* "Not every day or like I used to, but I'm drinking a lot. Even had a few blackouts. I'm obsessed with it. It's all I think about, all I want to do, can't say no to it."

"Well, some people can never drink normally. You might be one of those."

"But some days, a few times, I *was* able to drink just a few."

"I see. Are you still going to recovery meetings?"

"Every week."

"Does that help?"

"Sometimes. Some nights, I go out right after a meeting and drink."

"What else is going on?"

No fat pauses while she waits for me to uncover what I'm doing that's unhealthy. She doesn't have the time. I *know* I don't have the time.

"I got my master's, you knew that. Got a great job at the university. Not perfect, but it'll be great on my resumé. Doing a lot of mediation with one of my professors. I love that."

"Is drinking interfering with your work?"

"Never. But all that old stuff with men is starting again." I release a heavy sigh. "Dated a couple of guys, one for several months. He was really sweet. Then last week-end ..." *Gotta be honest.*

"Promiscuous behavior?" She says, matter-of-factly, which makes what I did sound more civilized than having sex with a stranger when he says hello. Or, in this most recent instance, when he says, You gettin' on the bus or what?

"Yeah," I mumble. "I had a blackout and went home with a complete stranger."

"Are you okay?"

"Well ... he assured me he wore a condom, if that's what you mean. And he didn't kill me."

Now there's a long, fat pause.

"I'm miserable," I say. "I can't believe I did this again. What the hell is wrong with me?"

"Do you remember why you did things like this in the past?"

I'm processing this. Over the many years I saw Miriam, I came to understand this part of my behavior, quite well, but lately, all of that self-awareness seems to have slipped away. "*Hmm ... I guess I'm ... trying to make myself feel worthwhile?*"

"Tell me some more about that." Yep, she's gonna make me figure this shit out. Again.

"I hate myself. Just like before. Actually, just parts of me. I really feel good about work."

"What about women? Have you made some friends out there?"

"I do have a couple of girlfriends, neighbors who are in

grad school. I got the work and women thing figured out. Booze and men—not so good."

"How connected are you with the women? Because if you're not letting them know you, then you're lonely. Right? You have that emotional closeness?" I cringe at the words, which smack of my other favorites, "vulnerable" and "intimate."

The phone line hums. Two thousand miles of phone line, and she still sees right through me. I can see straight through me too, right into my lonely, wasted heart.

"I'm not connected. Not to my friends or that guy I dated. Or to people in the meetings. No one really. Not even Mom. We talk every Sunday, but she doesn't know I'm drinking. How'd I get back here so fast?"

I suspect Miriam knows the answer, but she remains quiet. Hating the silence and the emptiness in my soul that is glaring in all that quiet, I chuckle and say, "Thought you fixed me."

She doesn't chuckle. "We can try to work on things over the phone, but you might want to find a therapist out there." Cutting right to the chase, not a speck of humor. Probably has another client waiting. "Maybe a male therapist this time."

"Why? Men are my problem."

"That's why. We didn't address all your issues. If you find a good therapist, he could help you work through some of those on a deeper level. I think a PhD would be best, not an MSW or psychiatrist. Do you know of any psychologists out there?"

"Uh, no." What does she think I've been doing out here? "My friend's getting her PhD in counseling. She might know some."

"That's a great start. And you need someone with strong boundaries. You understand what I mean?"

The boundaries I'm familiar with are: how much to drink, how often and where. "Not really."

"Well, you can seduce just about any man—"

"*Hah.* Not true."

"Lynn, you dated a child psychiatrist when you were nineteen."

"Hey, *he* seduced *me.*"

"And that sixty-year-old therapist who was chasing you around?" I can just imagine her subtle, questioning smile.

"I didn't seduce him."

"Okay, but you could have."

"*Ickk.* He was *such* a lecherous, old guy."

"Those are the kind of therapists you want to avoid."

"How would I know if a therapist has good boundaries?" I recall a few doctors at the psych hospital where I worked who never said much more to me than, Good morning or Hi, how are you. Those were boundaries? I thought they didn't like me.

"You'll know. Trust your instincts."

My instincts have not been reliable lately, especially with regard to men. "I'm good at spotting a guy who *is* seducible. Not sure it works the other way around."

"Then march in there and say, 'My last therapist told

me to find someone with good boundaries because I can seduce just about anyone.'" *Now* she laughs. Shrinks are *so* hilarious. "You know what I'm saying? A male therapist could be good for you, but only if he keeps super clean boundaries. And it's fine to tell him you need that. How he handles the conversation could help you decide if it's a good fit."

"So, find a shrink who's all professional, never flirty? Who acts like one of those guys who's madly in love with his wife?"

"Exactly. Ask your friend for the names of a couple a PhDs in town and call them. Then do me a favor. Call me in a few weeks. Let me know how you're doing. Otherwise, I'll worry."

You know you're in sorry shape when someone worrying about you gives you hope.

TWENTY-SIX

The Morning After

Before I have time to search for a new shrink, James calls again. I've been avoiding him, off and on, for a week. I'm still trying to alleviate shame by turning that one-night stand into something else, though into what, I don't know. All I know for sure is that I'm circling the drain. Tonight, I'm putting an end to this with a good explanation for why I can't see him anymore. Making dinner for him is the only way I can be certain to avoid Shermer's, drinking or a tequila obsession.

He brings a twelve-pack of beer. Shit. I could say no to the beer, but don't. I'm condemned to drink when alcohol is around. Six beers—and who knows how many hours—later, I could say no when James starts kissing me, but don't. I could keep us out of my bed, but don't.

Once we're in bed, I'm fully aware of my mistake. There's never a good blackout when you need one.

The sex is awful because I have no connection with

this man. I barely know him, and we have nothing in common. Hell, I'm not even a bus rider—he pulled over, I hopped on. Now I'm waiting for him to hurry and hop off. I use all my best moves to quicken this part of our ride in the bed.

When he finishes—I wasn't even trying to climax—he goes into the bathroom to clean up. Jumping up, I get dressed and go to the living room, lest he thinks I want some snuggling or snoozing.

When he comes out of the bathroom, he looks stricken. Racking my brain, I can't imagine what I left laying out in my tiny bathroom that would be so devastating. He slides his hands down over his face, stretching his jaw open.

I'm thinking he also didn't enjoy our sex. Maybe he faked an orgasm too. I didn't know men could do that. "What? What's wrong?"

His hands are still framing his gaping mouth, and he stares into the distance, as if in a trance. He is freaking me out.

"What the hell is wrong?"

"The condom ... I don't know how. It tore. It was ... torn."

The world comes crashing down around me, shards of glass everywhere. "Are you fucking kidding me?"

Looking crushed, he slowly shakes his head.

My mind is reeling. When was my last period? No, no, no! This is not good. This can't be happening.

James is coming out of his trance and stares at me.

"Could you … you know, get"—I'm already nodding—
"pregnant?"

"It's a *horrible* time for a condom to break. The worst."
What the hell is the protocol for even having this discussion with a two-night stand?

He releases a forceful, prolonged sigh. "What d'you …
or what should we do? What do you …"

There's no question as to what I will do, not that it's
any of his fucking business. Or is it? "I'll go to the clinic
tomorrow and get a morning after pill."

"Okay. Okay." He nods, reassuringly, mostly to
himself. "What can I do? Want me to go with you?"

Less than anything. "No. It's not a procedure. Just a pill
that makes you start your period."

"Can I come over tomorrow evening? After you … after
you take the pill."

"I'll be fine."

"I wanna come over anyway."

This is very weird to be discussing such a serious
matter with a man I hardly know. Not recommended; zero
out of five stars. And what a miserable way to learn that
another condition for great sex is having it with someone
with whom I will not freak out if our birth control fails.

When James shows up the next evening, I'm feeling
reflective and moody. The thought of almost accidentally
creating another human being is sobering. Talk about
broken dreams. If this doesn't spotlight the shit-show that
is my life, I'm not sure what will. I need to end this two-
night stand with James. We will not have a third night.

James gives me an awkward hug and an even more awkward pat on the back. I'm not sure if that pat was meant as an, Atta girl. Way to take one for the team. Or maybe it was more like, There, there, now. What he finally says is, "You alright?"

"I'm okay. The whole thing is messed up." I'm not about to explain how I've always wanted to be a mom but can't seem to find the maturity or the stability or the husband, and that, furthermore, he doesn't fit my criteria for a husband.

"Can we sit out front? I wanna have a smoke." A cigarette sounds like a perfectly good escape. Don't I deserve one? But I know where one cigarette will take me: to the store for a full pack.

I drag my wicker loveseat out to the porch not expecting to feel any love. It's so small that our thighs are touching, but that's our only connection. We sit there for a few minutes, gazing out at the yard. He puffs away on his cigarette. I alternately try, then try *not,* to inhale the smoke wafting by me.

Fidgeting with his cigarette pack, James finally says, "What happened last night really fucked with my head too. Couldn't sleep. I know we've only been hangin' out"—good, he doesn't think this is a relationship—"for a few weeks, but ...." He takes another drag off his cigarette, exhales. I hold my breath, watching the promise of nicotine pass me by. He motions between us. "This just doesn't seem like it's goin' anywhere."

My cheeks flame with shock, disbelief, embarrassment, indignation—almost a straight flush, a red one, right across my checks. He is cutting me loose. The night after he almost maybe impregnated me, he is breaking up. Fine, we weren't having a relationship, still, he's dumping me. The bus driver is dumping me. Would he be doing this if I hadn't taken a morning after pill? Would he walk away and leave me to deal—

Wait a minute. I've been trying to extract myself from this situation since it started. Now I don't have to do anything. For once, I don't have to be the bitch.

He exhales a plume of smoke. This time, I inhale deeply. "I don't want some complicated thing," he continues. "Went through that last year when me and my girlfriend split up. I was headed to Alaska to work on a fishin' boat but took that bus job. Then you got on my bus." He gives me a wry smile, very Leprechaun-like. "I like you, but … doesn't seem like we have much in common. You know?"

No, I hadn't noticed. He takes another pull from his cigarette. Exhales. Again, I inhale deeply. "Well, I'm … I'm not …" I'm not what? What lie do I have? What bullshit will allow me to save face? Hell, why say anything? I don't want to mislead him and definitely don't want to change his mind. "I just shouldn't be involved right now."

He nods and crushes out his cigarette butt, along with it my hopes of a second-hand nicotine hit. "So, I'm gonna be takin' off in a couple weeks. Headed up to that fishin' boat."

I'm slightly jilted that he isn't hanging around for a

piece of work such as myself, but mostly I'm relieved. Also, I feel a little bead of happiness for him. Anyone taking off like that, into the mystery, to pursue a dream has to be admired. Turns out the bus driver *is* going places. "Good for you," I say. "That sounds awesome."

"I'll write when I get up there so you have my address and number. If you're ever up there, you got a place to stay. And I'll send you some smoked salmon. I make a killer brine."

With little more than that, we have another awkward hug—good hugs require connection, I think—and he's gone. Gone fishin'.

I didn't think life could get much worse than going home, drunk, with the bus driver until I almost accidentally got pregnant with the bus driver then was dumped by him. What a ride! I can't *wait* to see what's at my next stop.

TWENTY-SEVEN

Good Boundaries

Heather, without any questions or judgment, gives me the names of two PhD psychologists: Dr. Wagner and Dr. Hoffman. Hoffman is a roly-poly, full-bearded man, a youngish Santa. He is warm, approachable and kind of ... fatherly. That's good. Fatherly is good. Not *my* father but *a* father. Wagner is younger, clean-cut, tall and lean. Call me crazy, but he's much cuter than Santa. I know, I'm looking for good boundaries, but he won't be bad to look at while we're working through my issues with men. He also comes across a little more analytical than Santa. I like that in a therapist.

I give both of them the my-last-shrink-says-good-boundaries spiel. Neither of them are fazed, but Dr. Hoffman blathers on about the importance of building a therapeutic relationship. He wants to develop a relation-ship? *Geez*, we just met. Dr. Wagner agrees, rather formally, that boundaries are important and says it sounds like my previous therapist was a very good one. Ding, ding, ding. Wagner it is.

I begin weekly appointments with Dr. Wagner, who is very professional and reserved but easy to talk to. He's a good listener, very non-reactive. I give him the crash course on my background, hitting most of the highlights, really the lowlights, of my teen years. It doesn't take him long to hone right in on my drinking.

I explain how, sometimes, I go to a bar with friends and don't drink. Instead, I enjoy the evening counting everyone else's beers, constantly wondering if I should or could have just one. Or seven. Other nights, I describe to Dr. Wagner, I manage to have only a few beers, constantly wondering if I should or could have another one. Or seven. Some nights, I tell him, I drink full-on, hard and fast, no counting, no wondering, no limits. Always exciting to see what unfolds on those nights, I say to Dr. Wagner with a chuckle.

He blinks, straight-faced. This guy wouldn't know irony if it bit him in the ass. He asks how I regulate my drinking on those nights when I abstain or have only a few. This is a great question, which I have given serious thought to, but if I knew the answer, I wouldn't need a shrink. I have absolutely no idea, I tell him. It seems I don't have a choice of whether or not I drink. Or not much of a choice.

Compulsive behavior, he calls it. I rather like the sound of that, like a gambler who sells her house and moves to Vegas. Compulsive, as in unable to resist, unavoidable, without a choice. Yep, that's me and booze.

I'm surprised how quickly I open up with Dr. Wagner. It must be his good boundaries. Though it wouldn't hurt if he showed a little emotion. I'm not *that* unstable. Am I?

In his waiting room one afternoon, I'm flipping through a copy of a psychology journal, making a mental note to chat with Dr. Wagner about his magazine choices. On the next page, staring right at me, is a headshot of Lawrence Segel, the psychiatrist I dated when we worked at the same hospital. He was treating adolescent patients there, and I practically was one—an adolescent, not a patient.

I'm reading Lawrence's column, some psychobabble, with my mouth still hanging open, when Dr. Wagner sticks his head in the waiting room. "Ready?"

I close the journal, and my mouth, and follow him.

"That was weird," I say. "There's an article in that magazine by an old boyfriend."

"Out there?" He points at his waiting room. "By who?"

"Brad Pitt," I say. A confused look from him. He's really going to have to keep up. "I'm kidding. His name's Lawrence Segel."

"Yeah. He has a regular column in that journal." Now a look of disbelief. "You know him?"

Shit. He knows who Lawrence is? I thought it was a fluke chance that I picked up a journal with an article by him. I don't want to tarnish his reputation. Dismissively, I say, "Oh, we worked at the same psych hospital like ... *pffhh*, seven years ago. We're not in touch anymore."

"You said you two dated?" His brow is furrowed, skeptical, maybe wondering if I'm lying.

I regret saying anything. Maybe a lot of mental health professionals know who Lawrence is. I knew he became some kind of big-wig. What if Dr. Wagner starts blabbing to his colleagues about this? Hold on—therapist-client privilege. He can't tell anyone what I say.

"You could call it dating. We saw each other for about a year and a half. Then he left me"—I thumb toward the waiting room—"for that job."

Probably thinking I have abandonment issues, and he isn't wrong, he pops right into well-trained, neutral psychotherapist mode: brows relaxed, no smile or frown. "A year and a half is a long time. You two were pretty serious?"

"Uh, serious isn't the right word. Unhealthy. Strange. Sick. He was a *child* psychiatrist. Thirty-three at the time. I was the nineteen-year-old mail clerk. With a massive cocaine habit."

Dr. Wagner's face remains neutral, probably thinking that I also have father issues, and he isn't wrong. He gives me a please-go-on nod, only I'm not going to. Even with therapist-client privilege, I don't want to trash Lawrence's image. Besides, that relationship ended long ago, and I spent many hours on Miriam's couch grieving it.

There's only one part of my relationship with Lawrence that I need to go on about with Dr. Wagner.

"He's one of the reasons my last therapist told me to get a male counselor with really good boundaries."

Despite Dr. Wagner making leaps and bounds in my psyche over the next few weeks, he is focusing on my relationships with women, not men. I don't have a lot of time to waste here. I'm pushing thirty, didn't find a husband in grad school but still have my sights on a healthy, loving relationship—whatever that is. I'm seeing a male therapist to root out my remaining issues with men, to unearth those stubborn daddy issues that mess up my relationships with men, and he wants to talk about women! Well, technically, he asked about my friends, but I don't have men friends.

"What about them?" I say. "What do you want to know?" Tick, tock.

"Anything you want to tell me. You have some good friends? Close friends?"

"Define close."

"Someone you call when you have a bad day, when you're sad or—"

"Define sad." I'm getting testy.

He looks unperturbed and waits for me to continue.

"Why are we talking about women—I mean, friends? Those are the easy relationships. It's the men that are killing me!"

"Okay. Let's talk about men. Do you have a boyfriend?"

Touché. "No," I say, dejected. "I'm avoiding men right now. But that's why I need to work on them so I don't have to keep avoiding them."

"Why don't you tell me about the people in your life who you're ... who you really care about?"

I lay it all out. Mom, who saved my life and would do anything for me but whose heart I don't want to break again by being forthright about my current condition. The smattering of men who I would call father figures: Floyd, Warren, my godfather, Bob. My phone-friend, Logan, who might be the only person who honestly knows me but who I'll probably never see again because we live two thousand miles apart. Sunita and Heather, who I consider my best friends but who don't know me very well, though not for any lack of interest on their parts. Women I became good friends with when I was sober but didn't maintain contact with when I moved out west. A co-worker, Nicole, who I've been playing racquetball with a few times a week. A few friends from graduate school, mainly Samuel and Isabelle.

Okay, that took all of six minutes. Tick, tock.

"Those women you were friends with before you moved, what happened there?"

I shrug. "We drifted apart. Liz came out here to see me once. Lori and I talked on the phone a few times." I contemplate for a minute what happened because we were pretty close. "I started drinking, that's what happened. I didn't want to lie to them. So, I distanced myself." I cringe inside remembering the last time Liz left me a phone message. "Stopped calling them. Didn't see them when I went home."

He looks like he's thinking. Perhaps wondering how the hell he can help a mess like me. In the silence, it dawns on me that he brought us full circle back to the women. Sneaky. "Sounds like you had some good connections in the past," he says, choosing his words carefully. "And you want those again."

I'm not sure if that's a question or a statement. Either way, he makes it sound pretty elementary. I might have to explain how long it took me to start connecting with people in my early twenties. Hopefully, I haven't lost all that ground.

"Yes. I want relationships like that again. *Close* relationships"—I clinch my teeth—"intimate relationships. With women and men." I'm going all out here, nothing left to lose. "The problem is, my self-esteem is pretty much in the toilet."

"*Aha.*" He nods, knowingly, but I don't think his self-esteem (or his head) has been in a toilet lately.

"I don't like myself much these days. Makes it hard to get close with people." Of course, he would know this. But he better do something more than nod.

"Are there things you *do* like about yourself?"

Surprisingly, a few things come right to mind. "I'm good at my job. I'm very dependable and loyal. Okay, I lie to my friends—about using—but I'd do anything for them. My friends and co-workers tell me I'm funny. I'm smart."

"That's all great stuff. To build on this, the best way is to act in other ways you feel good about." Here he goes with the elementary stuff again, like he just slapped some sense into me. *Thwack! Just stop behaving like a drunken slut. There, you're fixed.*

"It's not that simple. Just behave better." I pause for several seconds. "Okay, it is pretty simple ... but it's not easy." I release a big sigh. "I'd have to stop drinking."

TWENTY-EIGHT

Let's Do This Again Soon

After Dr. Wagner and Miriam so subtly point out that I'm not connecting with women, I get to work on this right away. They're the experts, after all. If one shrink tells you something, you might be able to shrug it off. When two shrinks tell you the same thing, you better take a good, long look at it. Plus, I can't trust myself to get within a hundred feet of a man, so women it is.

As part of this effort, I invite Isabelle to go backpacking, and she suggests bringing Kim, a friend of hers. The more women the merrier, I think. It'll be good practice. This will be the first time I've backpacked with women, except for Heidi, the supervisor who trained me as a wilderness ranger.

Planning a backpacking trip is always exciting, as I study the topo maps, select the route and trails, plan my meals, fit everything I need to survive for a couple of days into a thirty-five-pound pack. All the while, I daydream what these mountains and lakes will look like, what things the wilderness will teach me.

In my trusty Geo Metro, Isabelle, Kim and I head into the Eagle Cap Wilderness. We gossip and laugh and bounce about on a pot-holed, gravel Forest Service road. I'm full of anticipation for the stillness and centeredness I always feel in the wilderness and eager to share a spiritual experience with girlfriends. The long, jarring road doesn't diminish my enthusiasm. In fact, Forest Service roads are symbolic: the rough journey to peace. A rite of passage. Literally.

"Fuck, man. Roll the windows up," Kim hollers. Forest Service roads are also, notoriously, the dusty road to peace. We crank up the windows, leaving them cracked a bit for circulation. We're high enough in elevation that it's cool outside. She still isn't satisfied. "Wish we had a Jeep or something with higher clearance."

I wish she'd stop complaining. I respond with mock indignation. "Hey, this Geo is legendary." I pat the steering wheel. "It's taken me up lots of wilderness roads and never a busted oil pan."

Being jostled around in the passenger seat, Kim looks at me skeptically.

"Have you done a lot of backpacking?" I ask her, my voice vibrating as we drive over a patch of washboard road.

"Twice last summer."

I'm starting to be a little skeptical myself—she better

know how to dig and use a cathole because there won't be an outhouse. Knowing that Isabelle has backpacked a lot, I glance at her in the rearview mirror. She shrugs; nothing bothers her.

The trail starts off soft and mellow, covered with a thick duff of brown fir needles that smells earthy, like mushrooms, like leaves and fallen trees becoming dirt again. If the cycle of life had a smell, this would be it.

Quickly, the trail becomes rigorous and steep, crossing over a roaring creek. Rather than take our boots off and tread through the icy water, we carefully hop across boulders that are slick with damp, spongy moss.

A few hours and six miles later, we drop our packs, pull out our food bags and start a campfire. Huddled around the fire, I dig out my Alaskan smoked salmon— courtesy of James, who did write and send me this salmon —salivating at the sight of it. Kim and Isabelle pull out not one, not two, but *three* bottles of wine. I'm not talking about leather boda bags of wine, these are full glass bottles of wine. My jaw drops open at the absurdity: all the precious weight and space taken up in their packs. And the glass! If they slipped and fell on their packs, shattered glass and wine would've been all over their sleeping bags, tents, food. Some lucky bear would've been in heaven to find us.

"You carried bottles of wine all the way up here?" I ask.

"Hell yes," Kim replies. "What better way to end a long day on the trail. One for each of us."

Isabelle nods eagerly as she twists a corkscrew into the

first bottle. *Squeak, squeak, squeak. Pop!* My body flinches with the noise. That is a sound I never thought I'd hear, and never wanted to hear, in the wilderness. An unnatural, man-made sound. An explosion. Isabelle pours wine into her plastic camping mug, and I catch a whiff of musty, fermented grapes. An aroma I never wanted to smell in the wilderness. She passes the bottle to Kim. *Glurg, glurg, glurg.* Her mug is now also sloshing with dark, red wine. An explosion. Dark red liquid all around. What a bloody mess.

The incongruity of this scene has me rattled. I come to the wilderness to experience the world face-to-face. I'm here to take in the untamed earth as it has been long before I existed and as it will be long after I'm gone. The idea of being wasted out here, not fully present and aware, is almost ... sacrilegious.

The wine, one bottle for me, also has me rattled. For starters, I don't like wine, and the red stuff always gave me the worst headaches, almost as bad as a champagne headache. Guess my body isn't made for the fine stuff; give me a strong, bitter beer or hard alcohol, preferably with a bite or a burn to it. Also, one bottle, five measly glasses— would that be three camping mugs?—is enough to light up my craving for booze but not enough to quench it. Then I'd be out here in the middle of nowhere without another drop.

Kim takes a swig—no point sipping wine when it's in a camping mug. After her delicate mug swig, she passes the bottle to me. That woman has her priorities straight. But do I?

To my astonishment, with absolutely no hesitation, I wave my hand in front of the bottle. "No thanks. I don't want any. Not out here."

Who the hell was that? All the times I drank for no good reason, all the times I drank alone in my apartment, all the times I had no intention to drink but still did, and I'm turning down alcohol out here where there's no harm that I could do to anyone or anything: no men, no cars, no bars. I am baffled. Of all the things I have sullied with booze and drugs, all the amazing opportunities I willingly traded for a high or for a slamming hangover, and I finally draw the line at spoiling the wilderness.

Kim doesn't press the wine on me, no doubt thinking, More for me. She carefully wedges the bottle between her and Isabelle's packs. Wouldn't want to break the bottle now; it's come so far.

Trying to ignore the wine and the increasingly purple teeth of my friends, I dig into my dinner. The salmon is smoky and salty and slightly sweet—very much like James —the rice is filling, my chocolate is bittersweet, my cup of tea is hot and strong. Hydrated and my energy replenished, I clean up my dishes and put all my food stuff into a bear bag.

Isabelle and Kim are slipping into the chatter of the tipsy, everything exaggerated and glorious, each of them jockeying to top the last person's story, their voices and laughter becoming louder and louder. There isn't a bird or animal left in earshot.

"I'm gonna go scout around for a tree to hang my bear bag," I say. "And look for a good spot for my tent. If you wanna give me your water bottles, I'll filter some water too."

"Aww, that's so sweet of you," Kim says, now all cheerful and enamored with me. "Thank you."

Isabelle hands me her water bottle. "Sure you don't want some wine?"

I want to scream, No, I don't want any. You're ruining everything. You're missing your chance to catch a glimpse of eternity. "Positive. I'm not much of a wine drinker."

"Knew I shoulda brought whiskey," Isabelle says.

Whiskey. Yes. That would be so much better.

With my hands full of empty water bottles and the filter, I head down to the stream, the sound of tipsy women becoming more and more distant. At the creek, gushing whitewater finally blots out their voices. I sigh with relief. Finding a flat spot along the creek, I pull off my hiking boots and socks, dipping my tired feet into the icy water. The last of the sunshine streaks through the trees, low and slant.

After several minutes, birds begin their evening chorus. I scan the patchy forest around me, birds flitting from tree to tree. I can feel the cool evening air settling down along the streambed and around me. Finally, I'm a small speck in this vast world, and all my cares become trivial and slip away. In the wild, I'm content with myself exactly the way I am. It helps that there are no mirrors here; it matters little how I look when I can't see myself.

If only humans were like most animal species, and we all looked the same. Seen one squirrel, seen them all. Those Catholic schools were on to something with their gray, drab uniforms, making all the kids unvarying in their appearance. That must level the playing field and also strip the kids down to what matters: their behavior, menacing or kind, vengeful or forgiving.

This is why I come to the wilderness: for my gray plaid skirt and scratchy, white blouse, for a reminder of how common I am in the world. Out here, I fit in the world. Out here, I like myself just the way I am. If only I could bottle this state of mind. Bottle it ...

That's it! No wonder I don't want to taint this experience with a bottle of wine. There are so few places where I feel this comfortable in my skin. Maybe in Miriam's office, but that was just once a week and any self-acceptance came after first plowing through a bunch of pain and angst. I feel this way around my mom, but I can't live with her forever. If I could bottle this feeling, if I could feel this way back in the world where all the people are, where all my fears and self-doubts are, maybe I wouldn't want to drink there either. Maybe then I could say no to alcohol.

Another wilderness ranger once encouraged me to take everything I learned from the wilderness with me wherever I went, to always carry it with me. At the end of that summer as a ranger, I promised myself that I would do that. But the further I went from the wilderness, everything I learned there and everything I felt there dissipated. I couldn't hold on to it once I was back to my regular life. And I couldn't live in the wilderness. There must be a way to carry this back into the peopled world.

In the fading daylight, I move upstream and filter water. Then I locate a level spot for my tent, a spot close enough to the stream for the rushing water to drown out any obnoxious, partying noises from my friends.

On my way back to the wine tasting event, I scan for a good tree from which I can hang my bear bag. I leave my water bottle at the base of the tree so I can find it when I come back. It's getting dark. I'll be hanging my bear bag by the light of my headlamp.

"There she is," Isabelle says when she sees me. "We're gonna come look for you if you didn't come back soon." Kim nods and holds her wine mug up in the air, toasting my return.

"That stream is so beautiful. Hung out there for a while. Soaked my feet. Found a great spot for my tent. You guys gonna put your tents up here?"

They look at each other. "Tents?" Kim says, and they both start giggling.

"Prolly just put our tents over there." Isabelle swings her hand back and forth over her shoulder.

Good. Don't want you stumbling into my solitude. "Well, I'm gonna go hang my food and check out the stars for a while. You guys need anything?" I assume they know how to hang their food out of a bear's reach. On second thought, they're pretty drunk. "I can hang your food with mine ..."

"That'd be awesome." Isabelle stumbles over to her gear and shoves her food and an empty wine bottles into her bear bag. Kim crawls, literally, on her hands and knees over to her gear and does the same, though a bit more sloppily and slowly. Isabelle is watching her, cracking up.

We're gonna have to do this again real soon.

I'm peeved to be taking care of two drunks in the wild, but the alternative is risking a bear encounter. No chance in hell I can deter a hungry bear with the little .38 Special in my pack.

It takes me several attempts to successfully toss a rock, which is tied to the rope on our bear bags, over a high tree limb. Then I pulley the bags off the ground and out of a bear's reach, tying the rope around an adjacent tree.

I haul my gear down to my cozy campsite down by the creek. Kim and Isabelle, oblivious to my coming and going, are hooting and carrying on and stoking the fire until their campsite is blazing like a car lot. Obviously, they're here for the starry skies too.

Leaving the rainfly off my tent so I can see through the top screen, I turn off my headlamp and lie back. As my eyes adjust to the dark, I see the Milky Way galaxy smoldering in the sky, silent and permanent and all-knowing. Everything that ever happened on this planet, the entire jumble of humanity, occurred right here in full view of the Milky Way. All the pain and anguish and killing. All the joy and ecstasy and sacrifice. All the hate. All the love. All the wars. Every birth and every death. All the drunken back-packers. The universe right-sizes me, as always, but tonight leaves me lonely.

Another important wilderness lesson: one of the dangers of backpacking alone, or with drunken friends, is being lonely. There were only a handful of times I sat with others—another ranger, Floyd, David—and gazed at a wilderness night sky. Those were profound moments, and I loved sharing them. When we were planning this trip, I assumed Isabelle and Kim would enjoy the wilderness as much as I do. It never crossed my mind someone could hike all the way up here to this untouched place and not be ... touched. I wouldn't miss this for anything, not even, apparently, for a bottle of booze.

But here I am, as usual, alone. A solitary speck of dust clinging to this crumb of Earth while the planet spins madly at a thousand miles per hour. I don't want to experience this alone anymore. I want to stare into the limit-less sky, into the face of my mortality, with people by my side—friends, lovers, if I'm lucky, a husband and kids.

Snuggled in my sleeping bag and getting drowsy, an awareness begins creeping into my mind, far away at first, like a distant, barely visible planet. I can't quite make sense of the unsettled ... not really thought, more of a consciousness. Slowly, an understanding begins to come into focus. This wilderness loneliness is what I feel every-where. I'm facing everything the world has to offer me—pain, joy, fear, hope, boredom, fun—alone. I've pushed everyone away.

Well, at least the stars are always up there no matter what is happening in my life. They were present as I stumbled through a white night in Russia. They're here now; what a way to celebrate me, *finally*, finding a part of myself that I won't sacrifice for alcohol. The stars are present even when they're not visible, like in the daytime or in a too-bright city. They're up there, waiting. All I need to do is find a dark place.

My eyelids droop but, for some reason, I open them again. Maybe to make sure the stars are still there as I drift off to sleep. In that split second, a shooting star slices across the sky—*Swoosh!* A brilliant streak of white, hot light, a flash, there and gone.

Guess *that* star won't be up there waiting.

TWENTY-NINE

Waiting

I n the morning, I hike up and down the stream in search of huckleberries but find none. I've got cinnamon and brown sugar for my oatmeal, which, in the wild, is a yummy breakfast. I always think I'm going to eat this stuff back home but never do. After my gourmet breakfast, I have a leisurely two cups of hot tea then pack up my gear.

From the location of the sun in the sky, I figure it's close to ten a.m. when I mosey into Isabelle and Kim's silent campsite. They're still in their polar fleece, hair pressed flat against their heads, bedhead style, sipping coffee and staring at the gray, cold ashes in the firepit. What these two need is some Russian Caravan tea. Too bad. I'm fresh out.

The morning always comes, whether you're ready or not. For once in my life, I'm the person with a clear head surveying the wreckage of the night before. I rather like this view. Much better than the view from the pit of a hangover. Having been in their condition many, many times, I understand exactly how they feel but can find no compassion. They better not hurl in my Geo Metro on the washboardy, pot-holed road down the mountain.

It's another two hours before they're willing and able to hoist on their packs. There's very little chatter from them on our hike out, which suits me. I'm listening to the chatter of a mountain bluebird that seems to be following us and the roar of a waterfall in the distance. Breathing in the citrusy aroma of the alpine fir trees and the vanilla scent of the pines, I'm soaking in the wild, determined to carry it with me this time.

When I fill Dr. Wagner in on my backpacking trip, I explain how thrilled I was that I said no to drinking and how disappointed I was with my friends.

"What were you hoping for?" he asks.

"Sharing something. A few laughs. The scenery. Stargazing. Not getting plastered."

"Did you share any of that?"

"Let's see. The ride up was okay. Isabelle and I were excited. Her friend complained the whole way. Hiking up the mountain was the best part. Nothing bonds you like suffering. Once they whipped out that wine … nothing. They were gone."

Dr. Wagner doesn't say anything, probably waiting for my statement to settle in.

"I know, I know. I've been doing that for years: drinking and checking out. That's why I can't believe how easily I said no."

"What do you make of that?"

I shake my head. "Drinking would taint the one thing in my life that's—this sounds corny but—the one thing that's sacred. So much of my life's been a shit show. Until I started backpacking. But being up there with drunks ruined it."

"So now what? Just go with friends who don't drink?"

Do I detect a hint of irony? Because the overlap between friends, backpackers and non-drinkers in my life equals zero. And he knows it.

"Well, there's my uncle. We go every year. Could find some other women, or a boyfriend, who likes it." I shrug. "Or just pick up some guy while I'm out there." I chuckle, in case he thinks I'm serious.

Dr. Wagner grins. He is making *such* good progress in our therapy sessions.

But maybe his little show of emotion isn't about my clever wit, maybe his grin is about my progress. Like he's proud because, for some inexplicable reason, I didn't crash and burn when someone said, You wanna drink? And in the face of my utter disappointment in people, women this time, I still choose trying to connect. I will not give up on finding backpacking partners. For once, I don't hightail it out of the human race and go into hiding with two cats and a twelve-pack.

Who is this woman?

Our discussion about my failed female adventure, and my threat to pick up strange men in the wilderness, serves as a nice segue into us *finally* talking about men. Having been in therapy before, I know my growth (and my therapy bill) is proportional to my honesty, so I dive right in. Plus, the clock is ticking—the biological one, not the one-hour therapy clock.

I'm not sure if all women's issues with men start with their fathers, but that's where I start. Over the next few sessions, I paint a vivid picture for Dr. Wagner of my quaint relationship with Dad. He suggests that perhaps my seven-year-old self didn't think she could live without her dad. That gentle analysis rips my heart wide open. It also sheds light on why I so desperately seek after men, particularly older men. Some small, young part of myself is just trying to survive.

Dr. Wagner and I then march through my previous relationships with men and the glaring patterns evident. Seeking approval through sex. Check. Seeking men that will never abandon me. Check. Never being vulnerable— Whoa there, Doctor Wagner, is that word really necessary? Never letting a boyfriend get to know my true self. Check.

As if not actively trying to fix my brokenness with men, I begin hanging out with Chris, a guy from my recovery meeting who also has a couple of months clean and sober. No such thing as a recipe for disaster, is there?

Chris has a dry sense of humor and is super intellectual though never finished his college degree (for the same reasons it took me eight years to get one). He takes great interest in my work and even reads my thesis. He is the only friend who ever asked to read it. And a week later, he comes back with a bunch of questions.

I teach Chris how to play racquetball, which I've gotten quite good at. The game is new to him, but he has no trouble keeping up because he is a serious cyclist. The man's thighs are massive and rigid, like tree trunks. But who's looking?

Chris is warm and attentive but never makes a move on me. This is maddening because we've become friends, and I'm really attracted to him. He doesn't have a girl-friend, is heterosexual and, unless my instincts have gone haywire, is attracted to me. What is the hold-up? Still, not even a goodnight peck on the cheek.

I talk about this frustrating situation with Dr. Wagner, about how Chris and I have been hanging out for a month but nothing is happening.

"Nothing romantically?" he clarifies.

Eww, romance. "Nothing. Hasn't asked me on a date. Hasn't kissed me. We just play racquetball, drink coffee and go to meetings. Sometimes after a meeting, we walk around town and talk for hours. About serious stuff. That's it ..."

Dr. Wagner gives me a knowing smile. Do they teach that look in PhD programs? His smile gives me a giddy anxiety because he must know something about me that I don't.

"What?"

"Seems like you two are getting to know each other. Maybe ... getting close?"

I ponder this. Sometimes I feel close to Chris. I'm comfortable around him. Neither of us have much sobriety but keep going to meetings; that early recovery struggle is bonding.

"How's that feel?" he asks.

"Good, I guess. I like his company. We have things in common. I kind of ... trust him."

"Sounds pretty healthy."

"But I'm so attracted to him."

"So, you want to get closer. Physically?"

I nod.

"Maybe he's not ready." He says, shrugging.

Incredulous, I glare at him. "What man takes longer than a woman to be ready?"

Another damned knowing smile. "Anything wrong with the way things are?"

"Yeah. I can't stand it. My attraction is so intense, it's hard to ignore. It's just ... there, between us. We don't talk about it, act on it. Nothing."

"You could try waiting." He stretches a hand out in the air, palm up, just tossing out an idea.

"Waiting?" I shake my head. "For what?"

Now he glances up at the ceiling, pensive. Or praying

for my poor soul. Looking back at me, he says, "For anything."

His words hit me so hard, it's like he reached over and slapped me. An edgy apprehension begins to fizz in my solar plexus, right between my gut and my heart, a place where truth seems to come from. But messages from here come softly so can get drowned out by the racket from my brain.

"For anything?" I say, perplexed.

"Yep. Just wait," he says helpfully. A couple of optimistic head bobs, like this is going to be fun. "Don't take any action or make any moves and see what happens."

The apprehension now flaring between my gut and heart tells me that waiting is *not* going to be fun. But as I sit with that uneasiness, it begins to morph into a warm knowing, an ember of truth that I don't want to ignore. My intuition, I think.

"*Pffhhh*," I exhale loudly. "Waiting really sucks. It puts things in somebody else's hands and out of *mine*. I don't like that. It's dangerous."

Dr. Wagner raises his eyebrows, an inviting, please-go-on expression on his face. He all but rolls his finger in a circular motion.

Only I'm not going to keep rolling on about danger. Back to the topic. "What if he never makes a move? He never asks me out, we never date or ...anything?"

He leans back in his chair. "I don't know. What would that be like?"

These shrinks really need to get some new material. "I

don't know how to, just wait. For a man. Or a drink. For anything. What do I do with all those feelings and urges?"

"Have you heard of biofeedback?"

I was thinking of medication. Hard core meds. "Uh, I don't know."

"It can be used for relaxation. Could help you cope with those urges. Help you learn to self-soothe."

Relaxation? I never thought of myself as tense, more as playful and lighthearted. And self-soothing sounds like masturbation. I got that one figured out. "So, you're saying when I act on my urges or cravings, I'm trying to soothe myself?"

"That's what compulsive behavior is. Basically. Using something to try to change the way you feel." Dr. Wagner pauses, as if he's afraid that he's getting out ahead of me.

On the contrary, I'm keeping up. Cogs in my brain are clicking wildly into place, gears spinning like mad. Changing the way I feel is *exactly* why I use drugs and alcohol—that's why they're called *mood-altering* substances. Worried? A few drinks or hits, and I'm relaxed. Sad? A few drinks or lines, instant happiness. Already happy? A few drinks or pills, even happier. My aim was always for that endorphin-fueled condition where every-thing was in place, all of life was perfect and I was fulfilled. I suppose that could be described as "soothed." I think of it as soaring. A five-drink buzz. Or one fat line of cocaine. Now *that* is soothing.

Dr. Wagner continues. "For people with addiction problems, those compulsions get out of control."

Ohh, I know out of control. I usually overshoot my target. My initial craving is rarely satisfied with a few of anything. Like opening a bag of jalapeño potato chips to eat a few. *Okay, just three more. Hell, one more handful.* Then the serious bargaining begins and before I know it, I've eaten the entire bag and promise to skip dinner. This is what Rebecca, from my twelve-step meeting, meant when she said she was one drink away from a frat house. That first drink ignites the craving then all bets are off.

"Not just the drinking and drugs ..." I hesitate to finish my sentence, "but also smoking, overeating—even the men?" I grimace. "All just compulsions? Trying to feel better?"

"Or to avoid uncomfortable feelings. Stuffing them down."

A spool of relationships plays out in my mind, me feverishly—compulsively, I guess—trying to ensure that each man I pursued desired me or adored me or loved me. Always consumed with getting or keeping a man, being whoever I thought each man wanted me to be, losing sight of who I was. Losing control.

"I've always based my worth on men, but you're saying ... pretty much, that I use men like"—air quotes—"mood-altering substances?"

We stare at each other for a few beats. Maybe Dr. Wagner isn't keeping up. Then he gives a shoulder-to-shoulder head wobble. "More or less."

Perfect. All this time, I've been getting high on men. Snorting men: one out of five stars. Not recommended.

THIRTY

Leaps and Pounds

Through my new self-awareness that Dr. Wagner has so generously bestowed upon me, I see that almost all of my fun is just compulsive behavior. I can use just about anything like a drug. Once, I was so jealous of some attractive woman—an anorexic model or someone my then-boyfriend thought was hot—I went through a McDonald's drive-through and ordered a day's worth of calories. *I'll show her.* Like any good drug, while I was anticipating my food, then savoring those all-beef patties with special sauce, munching the salty fries, chasing them with a creamy, chocolate milkshake, I was no longer jealous. I was content and fulfilled. The jealousy returned shortly thereafter, at which point I felt utterly empty. Never felt so stuffed and so empty at the same time. Assault eating—*so* effective: stuffing your face and hoping some other woman gets fat.

At my next appointment, I ask Dr. Wagner if there is

any hope for me, though this new self-awareness already makes me feel less crazy.

"No quick fixes, sorry. But we could try some biofeedback. It could help you cope with those compulsions. Research shows if you can get some time between an urge and taking action, you have a better chance of resisting."

"Alright. I'm game for this biofeedback stuff. I'll try anything."

Dr. Wagner has me follow him into a small room adjacent to his office and explains how the biofeedback process works. I'll have a monitor on my finger, and he'll be talking me through a guided imagery exercise and watching my heartrate, my breathing and body temperature on a screen. He is very thorough about the whole thing, making sure I'm relaxed, letting me ask any questions.

No slapping me around with hard truths this week, huh?

He clips the monitor onto my finger and tells me to make myself comfortable in the recliner, which I push back slightly. I'm not about to splay out here, eyes closed, no matter how good his boundaries. It's not like I brought my gun. I stare at a tree outside the window, while he starts off with, "Focus on your breathing ..." So, I breathe, in and out, in and out. "Now, think of a place where you feel very safe, very comfortable ..." Instantly, I'm in Miriam's office. As he continues to talk, his voice is steady and calm and soothing. Eventually, I let my eyelids close but remain aware of the rhythm of my breathing, the cadence of Dr. Wagner's words. I'm not hypnotized; I'm fully conscious but dreamily relaxed. It's like being snuggled in my warm sleeping bag looking at a dazzling, starry sky. Or floating in my childhood pool watching cotton-ball clouds glide overhead, not a care in the world.

I'm not sure how long I'm in this tranquil state when Dr. Wagner gently guides me back to reality. It's disappointing to be back. I enjoyed not having a care in the world.

"How do you feel?" he asks.

"Great until you brought be back. My body feels kind of floppy, like I'd fall over if I stood up. A little drowsy." Leaning forward, I bring the chair back to an upright position. "Did it do something?" I say, pointing at his monitoring screen.

"You responded really well."

"I responded? Felt like I was completely out of it."

"That's the point. It tells us that you can get your body relaxed and regulate your body's responses—slow your heartrate, your breathing. That means you can do the same thing with your thoughts."

This man clearly has no compulsive behavior, never had a family-size bag of potato chips for lunch or stood in front of the freezer and ate a pint of ice cream. Or maybe he's hooked on porn? Nah—boundaries are too strong.

"I don't get it. I'm supposed to just control my thoughts? If I could do that, I would. And wouldn't be sitting here. No offense."

"What I'm getting at is you're able to relax your body,

and probably your thinking too, very easily. Most people can't do that so quickly in the first relaxation exercise."

Oh, I do like being the best at things. But relaxation?

"You look skeptical," Dr. Wagner says.

"Can you cut to the chase because I don't get how relaxing will help me not drink or seduce a guy—or not seduce. You know what I mean."

"Okay. You get an urge, you take action." He snaps his fingers. "We're trying to build your tolerance for not acting on an urge. With time, it'll get easier to resist them, to tolerate the feelings that make you want to escape."

Thwack! There he goes again. Like a slap, the word "escape" rings loud and clear and true. And stings. Changing feelings, avoiding feelings, stuffing feelings— sure, I guess. But escape, that is what I've been doing since I was a teenager, since the very first time I got high. Do I want to face my disappointment and heartbreak and lone- liness and anything else life throws at me? Turn and face my rotten self? No thanks. I always turn and run.

"How long?"

Dr. Wagner looks confused. "For?"

"Before it gets easier." Still a confused look from him. "For me to resist the urges."

"Good question. I'm not sure."

"But I can—what did you call it?—build my tolerance? For being uncomfortable?"

Definitive head nodding. "I think you can. You should probably keep going to twelve-step meetings too."

"Do I have to get one of these thingies?" I wave my

hand at his screen and the finger monitor. I imagine going out for coffee with Chris wearing a finger monitor. Every time I get the urge to jump his bones, I'll just close my eyes and focus on my breathing. That should get him turned on.

"You don't need a biofeedback machine. We'll do more relaxation here, but the idea is you learn to calm your system down. Slow your breathing, quiet your thoughts. It helps to find new behaviors, healthier ones, in place of the old ones. Everybody has hard times, feels bad. What's important is how you cope."

Booze *is* my coping mechanism. When I'm straight, I feel like I'm barely holding everything together, squeezing tighter and tighter, while inside pressure keeps building. Of course, every time I pick up drink, or a man, it's like yanking the pin out of a grenade.

"Coping, huh?" My eyes start to well up. Not helpful.

Dr. Wagner waits. If he doesn't say something, I *am* going to cry. Or leave. I glance at the clock. Ten minutes left. He's still waiting. Must've done a lot of biofeedback.

Tears slide down my cheeks. "I should know all this. Using booze and men to make me feel better doesn't work. I dealt with all this before." Frustrated, with my backsliding and my tears, I snatch a tissue and wipe them away. "Guess it didn't stick cuz I'm right back where I was eight years ago. The first few drinks feel good, then I'm gone. Drunk. And the men ..." I shake my head in disgust.

"How'd you feel when you were sober before?"

"Great. Well, not the first year. Definitely the last four."

"And how'd you resist drinking then?"

"With a lot of help."

"From?"

"Miriam. Mom. My friend, Logan. Lots of recovery meetings." I release a big sigh. "I don't do that anymore."

"Go to meetings?"

"Connect with people. Let them help me."

"*Ah*, yes. Relationships are hard."

"I don't let people in. Got that from my dad. That psycho boyfriend didn't help either." I stare out the window for a moment, until I get one of those bizarre visual fantasies about yanking it open and jumping. Talk about escape. This is only the second floor; probably just break my ankle. "You know, I work as a mediator, helping other people. Can hike over a ten-thousand-foot mountain pass carrying everything I need to survive for five days. But I have to learn how to have relationships. Don't kids learn this when they're like, five?"

Shaking his head, he says, "It's not easy. It may be harder than hiking over a mountain. But you had connections in the past. So, you just need a little refresher."

I take it as a compliment that Dr. Wagner isn't compelled to point out that my drinking is always going to take me straight back to kindergarten.

☙

My friendship-that's-not-getting-physical with Chris provides ample opportunity to practice new behavior and waiting. Before I go to meetings where I run into him, I stop touching up my hair and make-up. After a meeting, I don't invite him out for coffee, waiting for him to ask, which he usually does. Before I meet him at the racquet-ball courts, I don't check how my ass looks in that pair of shorts. Such progress!

I become aware of my self-soothing behavior every-where, as if I'm watching myself in a movie. I vie for my co-workers' adoration, for my clients' approval, to be the best writer Don and Warren have ever known, hell, the best writer who ever came through that university. But the more I refrain from acting on any of my urges or old behavior, the more relaxed I become around everyone, even Chris.

Slowly, I come to understand that my friendship-that's-not-getting-physical with Chris is what most people refer to as a "friendship." Normal male and female friends do things like hang out and talk and have coffee and play racquetball. They don't kiss goodnight. Ever. Who know? I guess this is friendly love.

I'm growing by leaps and bounds here. Leaps and bounds.

THIRTY-ONE

The Missing Pages

After several biofeedback sessions, even my brain and that naïve butterfly are calmer. None of this is a surprise to Dr. Wagner, who starts spouting off about biofeedback and cognitive behavioral therapy. Whatever. I'm just enjoying any relief I can get from the swamp of obsession and a lifetime of escaping.

On the outside, I'm sure no one notices anything different about me, but inside I am liberated. I'm not jumping at any and every opportunity for validation. At work, I'm still a good mediator, better, as I gain more experience, but I'm not fixated on wowing everyone. I prepare for my mediations, show up and use all my knowledge and skills to do my best work and go home.

With the help of Dr. Wagner, his relaxation machine and recovery meetings, I stitch together several weeks of sobriety. I'm excited but guarded; I've had this much time before. As an added measure of security, I stay super busy.

On weekends, I go hiking or get together with Heather or Sunita or play racquetball with Chris or Nicole. I pay attention to the men around me but don't take any action and don't try to force any outcomes. Each day I feel better about myself, and life starts to feel stable and comfortable. Though this sounds rather boring, surprisingly, I'm having fun. But I'd be lying—which wouldn't be so unusual—if I said I never thought about drinking.

The fantasy of alcohol is still in the periphery of my mind. Often, I remind myself that this fantasy is actually a nightmare disguised as a fun time. Most days, I can push those delusions out of my mind, but that pesky nightmare still lurks nearby, like behind me and to the left. If I turned quickly, I could almost catch a glimpse of the beast. On some days, it feels as if a living, breathing force is ready to pounce. I try not to look over my shoulder.

I attend recovery meetings frequently enough that I become a regular, even go early to connect with people other than Chris. I'm invited—a sure sign that I'm a regular—to a twelve-step book study with a group of women at Kitty's house. If someone devised a plan to trick an addict, who's just been yanked from the inferno, to work on healing herself, what better place than at the house of a woman named Kitty. Of course, I refrain from going until after the third or fourth invite because there will be women I don't know and some of the recovery literature is archaic and blah, blah, blah. Basically, I'm too chickenshit to open up with a bunch of women. Get naked with a strange man? No problem, where is he? Start getting honest with some women? Lemme think on that one.

When I finally get up the nerve, I know all the women there, and I talk, listen, laugh, get somewhat honest and, dare I say, emotionally intimate (cringe). Kitty and these women—Kitty and the cats!—teach me about staying clean and staying away from men and dealing with all the feelings that keep dragging me this way and that. They tell me one way to deal with them—feelings, not men—is to treat them like two-year-olds: don't let them drive the "car" but don't lock them in the trunk either. (On second thought, this might apply to men ...)

There is something unchaining about not worrying what these women think of me or if I sound wise or mature or funny or wondering how I look. These women are interested in being centered and right-sized, in seeing themselves as they truly are and not through the thick veil of intoxication. Being with them is a lot like being in the wilderness without a mirror.

Unlike so many times in the past when I sat in a meeting and my mind was elsewhere, I'm listening closely. Sometimes, I want to take notes but am too embarrassed to whip out pen and paper, so I pay close attention. To everyone. You have to because people in recovery, often people from whom you least expect to hear anything useful, spout things off, almost in passing, that are life-altering bombs of wisdom. And I never know which bomb might counter my brain's latest excuse to drink or do some other dumb shit. So, I stay fully present, and I'm taking detailed, mental notes at every meeting, like a court reporter—clickety, clickety, clicking away on my internal stenograph.

I think I found the missing pages of life's instruction manual.

There are days when the brain and the butterfly still get into a frenzy, stirred by some fantasy, and start in on me with persuasive talk and somersaults about fun and exciting opportunities that will destroy my life. When those two darlings start up, I remind myself fantasies are just that: make-believe, an ideal that is never as good as I imagine, a promise never delivered, a dream best not pursued. That's one sure way to ruin a perfectly good fantasy—act on it. I've also found it's best not to remain alone for long with the brain and the butterfly, so when they get into a tizzy about some pipedream, I call a friend or go to a meeting. Or I go on a hike or a walk or get outside—makes it harder for those two nut-cases to keep up.

Outside, I can always breathe easier, and I feel lighter, unburdened. I'm also closer to the Milky Way outside, even in the middle of the day, I know those stars are still up there. Outside, I remember the wilderness as if it is right next to me: the pungent smell of sagebrush, a mountain lion's chilling scream, the sweet-tasting water from an ice-cold stream. Outside, I can almost reach out and touch the stillness all around me, reminding me that everything is exactly as it should be. Reminding me that I can handle anything that comes my way—without a drink or drug. And that I don't have to handle everything alone, if I don't want to. Outside, I remember what matters. I remember I'm a speck of dust that will be here and gone in a flash.

When I have two months of sobriety, I'm on my way home from an all-day mediation during which I helped an organization out of a sticky conflict. I feel really good about my day, like I'm contributing something to the world and being a valuable member of society, for a change. Then a thought pops into my mind. *You know what would be great right now to really celebrate?*

Uh-oh, I think. I recognize that voice. I don't dare say, What would be great?

The miniscule part of my brain—a tiny, gelatinous holdout—that is *still* trying to kill me, goes on despite me not taking the bait. *A line of cocaine would be great. Mmwaah!* If my brain had fingers, it would pinch them all together, like a chef describing an exquisite dish, and kiss the slippery gray tips.

As soon as I enter my apartment, I drop my keys and purse, scratch the kitties' chins and call the other Kitty. When I hear her voice on the other end of that phone line, that line of mere sound waves and electricity becomes nothing short of a lifeline.

"*Phew!* Am I glad you're home. It's Lynn."

"Hey, what's up?"

"I got this craving for cocaine today. Outta the blue. Had a great day at work, been going to a couple of meetings a week, and I haven't snorted coke in like, ten years. It's not like I have a clue where to even score coke ... but I know where to find booze."

"I'm going to a meeting at seven. Why don't you come? I'll pick you up."

"That would be great."

"I'll pick you up early. Say, six-thirty?"

That's an hour. In the past, I've turned my life to shit in less time than that, but I can do this. I can go an hour without self-destructing, without a drink. And it would take me much longer than that to even find a source of cocaine in this town. Only sixty minutes. *Focus on your breathing ...*

At the meeting, I scan the room for any other familiar faces. No one I recognize, but there are the usual warm smiles. Then my eyes land on a man sitting a few seats down. Now, I'm not a dreamy-eyed, swoony type of gal, and I do *not* believe in love at first sight. I'm not even sure I believe in love. However, this Italian-looking man captures my eye. His dark hair is brushed back over his head, he has a strong, chiseled jaw and chin, even his jacket looks Italian: a soft, worn, light brown leather. He also wears a wedding band. That's too bad. But it's on his right ring finger, which is odd. Maybe he's left-handed and it gets in his way at work or something.

When it's my turn to talk, I don't even think about wowing anyone, not even the married, Italian man. That's how unnerved I am by this cocaine craving. Cocaine brought me to my knees when I was younger and, even on my worst days lately, coke was never an option. Even talking about it tonight is making me jittery. Plus, I'm practicing new behavior: *not* trying to impress people. I share all my crazy thoughts about wanting cocaine and how long it's been since I've snorted—the whole shebang. Minus the part about when I had my last drink, which, if I'm being honest (which I'm not), was only a couple of months ago.

I withhold this minor detail because I'm here to talk about cocaine, or so I tell myself. And also on the off chance that isn't a wedding ring on Mr. Italian's right hand because anyone with decent recovery wouldn't go out with a newcomer. Hey, at least I'm admitting to myself that I'm a newcomer.

When Mr. Italian, Steve, shares, his words also capture my attention, damn it. *He's probably married. Just focus on your breathing* ... He's been clean and sober for seven years and almost didn't make it, as with many meth addicts. Recovery is clearly a big priority in his life. That, and his family. *Nope, not dating me or anyone else.* He shares straight from the heart about struggling with being a good-enough father to two challenging kids while working full-time and finishing his bachelor's. *Jeezus!* I'm just trying not to go home with the bus driver.

This Thursday meeting becomes my favorite. It's a powerhouse group of people, most with multiple years clean and sober. They're light-hearted and quick to laugh at themselves, but, about staying off drugs and alcohol, they're deadly serious. After most meetings, several of us go out for coffee. Steve always includes me in conversations and asks how I'm doing, nothing flirty. Must be madly in love with his wife, lucky woman. Wouldn't you know it, I even like the way he smells: a faint woodsy scent, almost like cedar and a hint of warm leather from his jacket. He wears those canvas, high-top Converse tennis shoes. Red ones. How cool is that!

I shoot up a prayer to the universe that goes something like this: I wanna find a man like Steve—a man who'd be a devoted husband and father, hard-working, intelligent, smells yummy, wears cool clothes. And if it's not too much to ask, someone who cracks me up, loves the wilderness, is blown away by a starry night and isn't afraid of me and my past. Please and thank you. Immediately, I start drumming my fingers, thinking, Well, where is he? Huh? Huh?

Oh, right. Waiting. Always with the waiting. *Focus on your breathing ...*

Steve continues to show interest in my recovery but always with good boundaries. He only shakes my hand, no hugs. What perfect hands he has: warm, rugged, like he is no stranger to hard work, but not crusty and chapped like he's above using a little lotion. I like that in a man. *Oops, where was I? Ah, yes, boundaries.* My point being, boundaries aren't always well-maintained by people in recovery. That kind of stuff takes a long time for addicts and alcoholics to learn, but Steve seems to have that part of life figured out.

After one Thursday meeting, a few of us are standing around, chatting, and I ask Steve how things are with his daughter.

He gives a so-so hand wobble. "She's gonna graduate from high school. I was worried she'd drop out. And she's not hanging with her druggie friends anymore."

"That must be a relief."

"I'm still worried about her. Suppose that's part of being a dad.

"How's your wife handling it?"

He tips his head to the side and looks perplexed. "My wife?"

"Yeah, how's she handling things with your daughter?"

He shakes his head. "I'm not married."

THIRTY-TWO

Still Lying, Technically

My mouth falls open. I snap it shut. I swallow. "You're not?"

"We divorced a few years ago."

I'm all calm and collected on the outside, but inside I am leaping for joy and punching my fists in the air. *He's not married!* "Oh, I thought since you ... always wear that ring"—I point at his finger—"that you were married. I mean ... I noticed your ring the other day."

Glancing at it, he says, "This? I made it back in high school. First piece of jewelry I ever made." Then he gets the hint of a smile on his face. "Definitely not married."

"Cool. The ring, not your divorce." *He's not married!* "Is it made of silver?"

"Yeah, sterling silver."

He's not married! "So, you bend a band of silver or ..."

"I use lost wax casting. Carve the ring out of wax, then cast that wax model with silver."

He's not married! "So, you're a jeweler?"

"I wish. Just a hobby. I work on campus. And taking classes. Environmental science."

The universe heard my prayer. Do you backpack and love the Milky Way, I want to ask but think better of it. Let's not get carried away.

A few weeks after this conversation, Steve asks me out to a movie. He picks me up and, as I'm walking to his car, I notice someone else sitting in the back seat. This is interesting, I think. I'm glad I tucked my gun in my purse. Be prepared or be scared.

He meets me halfway up my sidewalk. "Hey, hope you don't mind, but ... uh ... I brought my son. He's not going to the movie with us. He's meeting some friends there. He's eleven so can't drive himself."

An eleven-year-old? What do I say to an eleven-year-old? "It's fine."

"Good. I wanted him to meet you." He pauses outside the passenger door. "Honestly, I thought it'd be more ... comfortable if he came too."

What a pair we make—he brought his son, and I brought my gun.

The three of us have a blast (my gun didn't, thankfully). His son looks like a younger version of Steve and is engaging and silly. Steve and his ex-wife sure did something right.

A couple of weeks later, I invite Steve and both his children over for homemade pizza. Kids and teens love pizza. Can't go wrong there. His eighteen-year-old daughter is a willowy beauty with full lips and striking eyes—I'd be worried about her too—but she's level-headed and focused on graduating from high school, even if a year late.

When I pull pizzas out of the oven, she giggles and says, "Dad *hates* pizza."

I glare at Steve, aghast, mouth open, eyes wide. "What? Don't like pizza! What kind of Italian are you?"

He gets all embarrassed and starts making excuses, how he only dislikes, not hates, commercial pizzas because they're so greasy and smothered in cheese, but he likes this kind of pizza—pointing at mine. I can't help grinning as he bumbles through all that. His kids are snickering and chowing down on the pizza. All the while, I am blissed out—stone-cold sober euphoria—because I love having this family huddled around my little dining room table, filling my apartment with playfulness and laughter and nudging their way into my heart. *I think I'd be a good step-mom.* Not that I'm trying to force anything here ...

Since Steve and I both have a long history of substance abuse, nothing about my past scares him. We share our horror stories, chuckling about the absurd ones and growing quiet about the nightmarish ones. I don't have to hide parts of myself from him, as long as I don't pick up a drink. There's no doubt in my mind that if I start using again, I can kiss Steve good-bye. In fact, if I tell him it's only been a few months since my last drink, he would kiss *me* good-bye. So, technically, I suppose I *am* hiding one teensy, tiny part of myself. But this is the most honest and genuine I've ever been with a man. I'm not giving him up. If this relationship goes somewhere, and I actually stay clean and sober, then I'll decide how and when to get honest.

In meetings, I use my old standby, saying, I'm not using *today*, which translates to, I haven't used anything for three months. When Steve asks how long I've been clean, I stretch the truth—fine, I flat out lie—and say eleven months. But who's counting?

Many times, I ask myself why I'm lying to this incredible man. What can I say? I lie because Steve is too healthy to date a woman with less than a year, and I don't think I can wait nine months. *Geez*, that's long enough to have a baby. *Wonder if he wants more children?* Yes, those nine months would be a perfect opportunity to practice waiting, but I'm getting plenty of practice by staying away from booze and bars and cocaine and even sex. I lie because people don't change overnight. Sometimes people never change. I lie because I'm an addict and my lips are moving.

In the midst of me technically lying, I get to know Steve. He works out at the gym three times a week; hasn't backpacked in years, since his kids were born, but always loved it; and has a weakness for a good apple fritter for breakfast (close enough to coffeecake). When he tells me that he doesn't like football, I ask him to marry me, chuckling so he knows I'm kidding and doesn't think I'm trying to force anything. I'm only partially kidding; I *really* hate football. He gives me a sidewise glance and chuckles too, but it sounds more like a nervous chuckle. *Wonder if he'd ever marry again?* When he rants about human dependence on fossil fuels and how solar and wind energy, alone, can massively reduce fossil fuel use, I'm ecstatic.

This is also when I become frightened. I'm frightened for so many reasons, mostly because Steve seems too good to be true, which means I'm missing something awful, like he has a side gig as a serial rapist. Or he hates cats. I'm scared because I'm not sure he likes me as much as I like him. I'm horrified that I'm lying to him, and he'll find out and dump me. And I'm petrified that he will rip my heart in two. For some mysterious reason though, I don't turn and run.

In my other relationships, even when my gut was telling me to end it, I talked myself into staying. All for logical reasons: he's a psychologist, he's becoming a psychologist, he needs a psychologist. But with Steve, I keep trying to talk myself *out of* this relationship, also with sound reasoning: he already has kids, he lives in a double-wide mobile home, he likes Frank Zappa. But despite all my logic, despite myself, we keep growing closer. I'm not sure if I'm falling in love, but falling is a good description of how I feel. Every day, I respect him and cherish him and lust after him more than the day before. We never run out of things to say, though sometimes, we laugh so hard we can barely talk.

Dr. Wagner doesn't act surprised when I tell him that I'm *still waiting*, postponing sex with Steve. Over a month,

I say proudly—that's so long. Dr. Wagner nods, all neutral-like. Guess he's not as impressed with my waiting will-power.

When I explain to Steve that I'm waiting on the sex part, he doesn't pressure me, which, of course, makes me immediately think, What? You don't want me? I'm not irresistible?

Oh, right. Waiting. *Focus on your breathing ...*

To his credit, Steve does ask why we are waiting. I love that he says "we."

"I have a history of jumping in the sack with guys too quickly, and that never works out. So, I want to make sure we know each other, that we're friends first. At least, until we think this might go somewhere." *Sheesh!* I'm like a born-again high school virgin. Well, as far as sexual maturity goes, I am basically fifteen. That's what happens when you start having sex way too young and for all the wrong reasons.

He nods. "I already think this might go somewhere. I really care about you. But I'm in no hurry."

That's too bad. "Plus, sex is more fun if you can talk about it," I say enthusiastically. "Know what I mean?"

He shakes his head, not looking too enthusiastic.

"When you're comfortable enough that you can just ... talk about it. What you like, don't like." This is the first time I've tried to articulate this personal guideline, so it seems like a little test, not of Steve, more like a test of us.

"I've never had that with a woman, but it sounds good."

I squint at him. "What, sex?" We both crack up.

Then, we proceed to have this crazily fun, honest discussion about sex, our likes and dislikes, our best and worst. It's a complete turn-on, but we still refrain from having sex.

After our sexy conversation, I'm resting my head on his chest—my head fits perfectly in that nook between his pecs and his shoulder—and his arm is wrapped around me. "It's not so much the sex I want to go slow on, it's the getting serious part. I want to be careful. When I have sex first, it always muddles everything up. I want some kind of sign first."

"A *sign?*" He lifts his head, looks around the room. "Give me some paper and a marker."

"I don't want to self-will this relationship. Force it to move in a certain direction." *Wonder if he's falling in love with me?* "So, I'm waiting for a sign that it's ... healthy. That we're a good match."

"And where will this sign come from?"

"*Hmm.* Good question. From god?" I say skeptically.

"Do you believe in god?"

"Not really." We have a quick laugh. "Seriously, I don't believe in the god I was raised with or any kind of personified being."

"Me neither."

"But I'm trying to believe in something other than what my brain tells me. This thing"—I tap my temple— "has proven very unreliable over the years. But sometimes I get, not a message—I wish it was that clear, a little sticky note—but a gut feeling or an intuition. Usually, I get it right here." I lay my hand on my solar plexus. "Not sure where it comes from. The universe maybe? But I try to pay attention to it."

"I kind of believe in the energy between all of us, between everything. Even animals—"

"Cats?"

"Especially cats," he says, smiling. This man is checking all the boxes. "I think our spirits form a collective, I don't know what ... some kind of power that we can tap into if we want. It's always there."

Like the Milky Way and the stars ... "I'm trying to tap into some intuition or sign from the universe about this." I motion back and forth between us. "Cuz I like you a lot and don't wanna blow this. But sometimes the universe can be really quiet. So, I'm listening and waiting."

He looks over at me, his eyes wide with mock surprise, his eyebrows shooting up. "I'm thirty-seven and you're waiting for a sign from the universe?" I love listening to this man laugh, his laughter coming up from deep in his chest, now floating all around me.

I'm grinning, ear-to-ear. "Yes! I'm waiting for something other than what comes instantly"—I snap my fingers—"from my brain." We kiss once, twice, then a lingering kiss. "Or my lust. My lust has also been unreliable."

Now his eyes are closed, but he opens them partway, all smoldering and sexy-like, and looks into my eyes. He looks aroused and serious at the same time. I hold his gaze, unafraid to let him see the real me (okay, most of the real me). Go ahead, look into my soul. It's not such a wretched place. And I'm pretty sure he can handle whatever he finds there. I hope he can.

"You know, I am kidding," he says. "About being thirty-seven and still waiting. I want this to work too. I can wait as long as you want." I like that in a boyfriend.

So, we watch for a sign from the universe. Together. We wait. Together.

Focus on your breathing ...

IF YOU NEED HELP

Find an anonymous drug or alcohol abuse recovery meeting, many are now held virtually.

Suicide & Crisis Lifeline: dial or text 988

Runaway Hotline: 1-800-RUNAWAY (786-2929)

Planned Parenthood: 1-800-230-PLAN (7526) or text "PPNOW" to 774636

Domestic Violence Hotline: 1-800-799-SAFE (7233) or text "START" to 88788

AUTHOR'S NOTE

THANKS FOR JOINING ME ON THIS WILD TRIP!

If you feel inspired by my journey, please tell a friend about this book and post a review on Amazon, Goodreads or your favorite online bookstore.

HIKING IN THE WILDERNESS

29753266R00177